SCUBA DIVE -
WHERE ROOTS MEET THE SKY

BOOK II

VEDANTA FOR CHILDREN

ARTHI KRISHNA

Clever Fox® PUBLISHING
Chennai • Bangalore

CLEVER FOX PUBLISHING
Chennai, India

Published by CLEVER FOX PUBLISHING 2025

ISBN: 978-93-7500-196-6

SANSKRIT TRANSLITERATION TABLE

Many Sanskrit words are written in English letters in the book, so you can read them easily, but English can't always capture the exact sound of Sanskrit. That's where the *transliteration table* helps!

It's like a sound map, showing you how each letter should really be pronounced and connect with its original vibration and meaning.

Vowels				
DS	**IAST**	**DS**	**IAST**	
अ	a	ॡ	ḹ	
आ	ā	ए	e	
इ	i	ऐ	ai	
ई	ī	ओ	o	
उ	u	औ	au	
ऊ	ū	अं	ṃ	
ऋ	ṛ	अः	ḥ	
ॠ	ṝ	ऽ	'	
ऌ	ḷ			

Consonants									
Velars		**Palatals**		**Retroflexes**		**Dentals**		**Labials**	
DS	**IAST**	**DS**	**IAST**	**DS**	**IAST**	**DS**	**IAST**	**DS**	**IAST**
क	ka	च	ca	ट	ṭa	त	ta	प	pa
ख	kha	छ	cha	ठ	ṭha	थ	tha	फ	pha
ग	ga	ज	ja	ड	ḍa	द	da	ब	ba
घ	gha	झ	jha	ढ	ḍha	ध	dha	भ	bha
ङ	ṅa	ञ	ña	ण	ṇa	न	na	म	ma
ह	ha	य	ya	र	Ra	ल	la	व	va
		श	śa	ष	ṣa	स	sa		

WHAT'S IN THE BOOK?

SCUBA Dive - Where Roots Meet the Sky is the second book in the SCUBA Dive series.

At school, you memorised chapters, formulas, and dates, but no one taught you how to manage overthinking, heartbreak, or identity confusion. This book is a life manual that takes you deeper into yourself... just without homework or surprise tests.

While the first book feels like learning to swim in the swimming pool of life, this book will feel like you are learning to swim in the depths of the ocean of life.

When you dive deeper into "who you really are," you naturally rise higher in life; grounded, fearless, and free.

From "Who Am I?" to "Where Am I?"

Your first dive, *Scuba Dive - Beyond the Mind*, asked you the most personal, profound question of all: Who am I? It introduced you to the real YOU, beyond the body and the mind.

But once you've met yourself... a new question naturally arises:

Where am I? What is this world I find myself in? What is my relationship with the world and the people?

Look around you. The stars, the sky, the people, the pain, the joy, the choices...

So much happens every day. But how much of it do we truly understand?

Have you ever caught yourself wondering?

- **Where did this entire universe come from?**
- **What's it made of, really?**
- **Why do people act so differently, even in the same situations?**
- **Does God Exist? How can I know God?**
- **Can I rise high, from complaints, confusions, grudges, regrets, blame and doubts to confidence, clarity, contentment and joy?**

If even *one* of these questions has whispered to you in the quiet moments,

Then this book is for you.

The answer lies not in the sky, but deep beneath, in your roots.

Just like a tree, you can only soar as high as you are rooted deep. Without strong roots, even the tallest tree falls to a passing wind. But when the foundation is anchored in truth, no storm can shake it.

What are the roots? The **timeless wisdom of Sanatana Dharma, the living current of Indian civilisation flowing through the Vedas, the Upanishads, the Gītā,** passed on through generations by the great mystics of Bharata.

But let me warn you, the book is not filled with easy answers.

Instead, it**'s packed with stories that make you wonder, chants that connect to the divinity in you, examples from real life, and wisdom that awakens!!!!**

The book is for the curious pre-teen, the questioning teen, the searching youth, and the reflective adult.

It's for anyone ready to begin a journey into the heart of the Vedas and Upanishads.

The stories you'll find here, especially from the Purāṇas, may seem mystical, even illogical at first.

But that's how the Ṛṣis designed them. Because truth isn't always understood with the mind. It is felt. It bypasses logic and speaks directly to YOU.

So...Are you ready to dive in with an open mind?

Are you ready to go beyond surface understanding? To question, to feel, to remember?

Take a deep breath... and dive once more... Where Roots Meet the Sky.

ABOUT THE AUTHOR & ILLUSTRATOR

ARTHI KRISHNA

Arthi Krishna began her career in the IT field and later moved into teaching, where she found her calling in working with children and young adults. She has been associated with Chinmaya Mission for over 15 years, conducting classes for children to imbibe values through stories and the Bhagavat Gita.

As a Life Coach and Golden Period Educator, she works with individuals, especially youth, to empower them to master their minds, make thoughtful choices, and develop confidence, self-reliance and resilience.

She also practises natural farming at her family farm, **SANKALPA farms**, where she promotes simple, sustainable living through community efforts.

Arthi believes that when we understand and live in tune with our own nature, we learn to live in harmony with the world around us.

VAIISHNAVII ARUNKUMAR

Vaiishnavii Arunkumar, a Class 9 student, has been attending and enjoying Balavihar classes since Grade 1, where she has learnt value-based concepts of life from the Bhagavad Gita. Vaiishnavii actively participates in Bhajans and Shloka recitations and has a deep passion for Art and Music. In her free time, she enjoys Painting, Singing, and Learning the keyboard and Guitar (for Carnatic Music).

OTHER BOOKS BY ARTHI KRISHNA

SCUBA Dive - Beyond the mind is the first of four books in the SCUBA Dive series, bringing out the wisdom of Vedanta for children in simple related ways through stories, Bhagavad-gita chants and anecdotes from life.

ACKNOWLEDGEMENT

Scuba Dive - Where Roots Meet the Sky was born from years of listening to the Śāstras, to the words of many Gurus, and to the silences in between. Each teaching has been a drop, slowly filling the ocean of understanding within.

This book brings together reflections and learnings drawn from the path illuminated by the Śāstras. It is shared with the intention that these insights may be of value to others who seek clarity and direction.

The wisdom of my teachers has shaped how I see the world, turning questions into reflections, and reflections into gentle transformations.

The words of Pujya Gurudev Swami Chinmayananda have been a steady light on this journey:

"Service of the country is the service of the Lord of Lords, and devotion to the people is devotion to the Supreme Self."

The book is a small attempt, a little squirrel-like offering of gratitude, wonder, and love to the rich heritage of Bhārata, and to all the Gurus who dedicated themselves to keep this wisdom alive and relevant through every challenge.

Om Gurubhyo Namaha. The Guru shines through all.

To all those who helped make this work possible, through editing, illustrations, reviews, language, design, and every unseen act of support, and to my family, friends, well-wishers, and readers who have walked this journey with me since "*Scuba Dive - Beyond the Mind*", my heart bows in gratitude.

Lastly, I offer this book to my country Bharata, the cradle of this profound knowledge and civilisation and to the Supreme, the Source and the Sea, from whom all arises, and into whom all returns.

Om Tat Sat

FOREWORD

"Where Roots Meet the Sky" is a very attractive and catchy title for the book SCUBA Dive. The specialty of this book lies in its inclusion of many important Sanskrit verses. The lofty ideas of Sanatan Dharma have been presented in simple, easy-to-understand language, and the topics chosen are of contemporary relevance. Instilling the idea that society is an extension of the Self, even at a very tender age, is a valuable contribution to the growth of children. I wish dear Arthi all the best for bringing this wonderful book into the world.

-Yogashree N V Raghuramji, YogaBharati Foundation

Blending the timeless wisdom of Vedānta with the curiosity of the modern mind, this work speaks to readers across ages.

In an age where attention is fragmented and wisdom is often reduced to soundbites, SCUBA Dive - Where Roots Meet the Sky restores the art of reflection. It rekindles wonder, the sacred curiosity that lies at the heart of learning. Its questions - Who am I? Where am I? Why am I here?, are living gateways to transformation.

This book will not only make readers think; it will make them feel the quiet joy of rediscovering themselves amidst the noise of the world.

Our wishes and blessings to Arthi Krishna Ji and her wonderful team that created this book. May more and more experience curiosity, peace and happiness through these books.

-Siddhayogi Adinarayanan and Matrushree Ananthalakshmi

Anaadi Foundation

The use of anecdotes and stories from various sources - both ancient and modern makes the book joyful to read and the concepts in it very easy to understand. May this book reach as many people as possible and bring a transformation in their lives.

-Swami Aparajitanandaji, Chinmaya Mission

CONTENTS

1. The Magnificent World!! 1
2. Vasudhaiva Kutumbakam 8
3. The World Is a Dream 18
4. Perception to Reality 29
5. Big Bang: A Myth 39
6. Singularity to Plurality 53
7. The Universe is Ever Changing 67
8. The Parallel Universes 80
9. Empowering Freedom 95
10. Pralaya-Dissolution 117

Nasadiya Sukta of Rig Veda 129

Conclusions 131

CHAPTER 1

The Magnificent World!!

Let us start this chapter with a question: **What does the word WORLD mean to you?**

Does it mean the planet, trees, rivers, continents inhabited by people?

The Sanskrit word for world is *Jagat*.

Where is your home in this Jagat?

Now, I live in a house.

This house is part of a society.

The society is part of a district.

The district is part of a city.

The city is part of a country.

The country is part of a continent.

The continent is part of Mother Earth.

The earth is part of the Solar System.

The solar system is part of the Universe.

The universe is part of a Multiverse.

Just Visualise:

Read this. Then close your eyes and picture yourself through a camera. Visualize yourself moving away into space, beyond the city, beyond the country, beyond Earth, beyond the planets of the solar system and the stars, out into space, into vastness. How does it feel to be part of such a vast Universe? Do you feel expansive, insignificant, or both?

Now, we all know that the universe is really big; beyond our imagination!!!!!

But the ṛṣis of Bhārata had a vision of this.

How big is this universe?????

Let us explore the Universe through the eyes of the ṛṣis.

THE SPACE TIME MAP

How do you think astronauts on a different planet would identify our location on Earth? They would locate us through the latitude and longitude.

The Global Positioning System (GPS) can identify your location in space and time with the help of satellites. In addition to latitude, longitude and altitude, the GPS provides a fourth dimension-TIME. Hence, the GPS uses 4 dimensions for identifying the location.

The **ancient seers or the Guru Positioning system (GPS) envisaged Space or Ākāś as a living organism, its many cells as multiple universes**, with each universe being immensely vast.

THE VEDIC GPS MANTRA

The seers have given a GPS mantra to locate our existence in this Space-Time.

Every universe in the multiverse has a creator, preserver and destroyer intelligence as Brahma, Viṣṇu and Rudra.

Brahma, the creator intelligence, lasts for 100 years and hence the **life of the universe is said to be 100 Brahma years.**

Now!!!! These 100 years are not the same as human years.

Time is different on other planets compared to earth. For example, a day and a year are longer on Jupiter than on earth.

For some insects, one human day can be their entire lifetime. The insect would have lived, slept many times, eaten, procreated and died in one human day.

So, let's understand that a **human's timeline is like an insect's timeline in contrast to Brahmā's timeline**.

Here is an example of the GPS mantra. It is a Saṅkalpa mantra that changes according to the geographical location and time. It includes the time coordinates and the space coordinates. The purpose of the Saṅkalpa mantra is to announce the presence of a person in relation to time and space coordinates:

"Om Viṣṇurviṣṇurviṣṇuḥ. Śrīmadbhagavato Mahāpuruṣaśya Viṣṇōrājñayā Pravartamānasya Adyaitasya Brahmanōh Dvitīye Parārdhe Śrīśvetavarāhakalpe Vaivasvatamanvantare Aṣṭāviṁśatitame Yuge Kaliyuge Kali Prathamacharaṇe Bhurlōke Bhāratavarṣe Jambūdvīpe Bhāratakhande Āryāvartāntargatabrahmāvartasya (Place) Kṣētre..."

Here's a breakdown of what a Saṅkalpa mantra typically involves:

- Invocation to God:

Starts with an invocation to a specific deity, such as Lord Viṣṇu.

- Cosmic Time Reference:

Declares the current age of the universe according to Vedic cosmology, including the era of Brahma called kalpa (**Śrīśvetavarāhakalpe**), the age of the manvantara* (*Vaivasvatamanvantare*), and the time within the current mahayuga* (*Aṣṭāviṁśatitame Yuge Kaliyuge, 28th mahayuga*), the Kali Yuga.

- Geographical Context:

Mentions the specific location where the ritual is being performed, such as Bharatavarsha and Jambudveepa, Bharatakhande.

According to the Vedas, the current age of the universe is - 155.52 trillion human years.

The total age of the universe is 311.04 trillion human years (which is equivalent to 100 years of Brahma).

This story from the Devī Bhāgavata Purāṇa will help us understand the expanse of the Universe and much more.

*A yuga is a cycle of four ages (Satya, Treta, Dvapara, and Kali) that make up a Mahayuga of 4,320,000 years. A manvantara is a larger cycle, consisting of 71 Mahayugas, during which a specific Manu is the progenitor (first ancestor) of mankind, along with a set of Saptarishis and demigods. Both yugas and manvantaras are part of an even larger cycle called a kalpa, which is one day of the creator god, Brahma.

DEVĪ IN MAṆIDVĪPA

A STORY FROM DEVĪ BHĀGAVATA PURĀṆA

Devī Ādi Parāśakti, who is the primordial Mother of the Universe, i.e., the creative dynamic force that gives rise to the universe, once appeared to the Trinity- Brahma, Viṣṇu, and Maheśwara. She said, "It is now time for creation."

Brahma, who is the creator God, needed the raw materials for creation. Devī immediately summoned a bejewelled vimāna (a flying vehicle). The vimāna was studded with colourful precious gems. When the trinity got onto it, it shot off into space. They saw the rivers and the mountains fade away. They passed through the Gandharva Loka, the Indra Loka, and the Lokas of the ṛṣis.

Then they reached Satya Loka. There, they saw Lord Brahma sitting on a Lotus with Devī Sarasvatī. Viṣṇu and Maheśwara were surprised to see Brahma in the Vimāna and also in Satya Loka (Brahma Loka) at the same time.

Next, in the blink of an eye, they reached Kailāśa. There, they saw Lord Śiva, sitting on his bull Nandi, along with Devī Pārvatī, and Gaṇeśa and Kārtikeya standing with their parents. Viṣṇu and Brahma were surprised to see Lord Śiva in the Vimāna as well as in Kailāśa at the same time.

Then, as quick as lightning, the vimāna took the trinity to Vaikuṇṭha. There, they saw Lord Viṣṇu, reclining on the Ādiśeṣa, surrounded by the Cosmic Ocean, and Devī Lakṣmī accompanying him. Brahma and Maheśwara were surprised to see Lord Viṣṇu in the vimāna and in Vaikuṇṭha too.

Next, they reached a Dvīpa (Island), glittering like it was studded with precious gems. The Dvīpa was encircled by seven oceans. The vimāna flew past the oceans and stopped at the island. This was the Mani Dvīpa, the abode of Devī Ādi Śakti.

She sat on a pedestal in a red garment. She looked magnificent. The Trinity approached her. As they got closer, they saw in the nail of the big toe of the Mother Goddess, rivers, mountains, the gandharvas, ṛṣis, Indra, Brahma Loka, Kailāśa, Vaikuṇṭha; they also saw many Brahma, many Viṣṇu and many Maheśwara.

They prostrated at the feet of the Mother Goddess. Mother Goddess said to them, "I will give you my Śakti so that you three can perform your duties of Creation, Sustenance, and Destruction of the Universe". From Devī 's Sattva guṇa came Goddess Sarasvatī, who became the Śakti of Lord Brahma. From Devī's Rajo guṇa came Goddess Lakṣmī, who became the Śakti of Lord Viṣṇu and from Devī 's Tamo guṇa came Goddess Pārvatī who became the Śakti of Lord Śiva.

With a gracious look, the Divine Goddess said:- "O Brahma! O Viṣṇu! O Maheśwara! Now that you have my Śakti, do your respective works of creation, preservation, and destruction of the Universe; create your abodes, and live in happiness."

This story brings out the vastness of the universe.

Brahma, Viṣṇu and Maheśwara being present on the vehicle and also in their lokas at the same moment, signifies the multiple universes with each universe being governed by the creative, preservative and transformative forces.

The age of the universe is 155.52 trillion human years. The life of the multi- universe may be much more....

Points to ponder: -

- Why did the Trinity see themselves on the vimāna and in their respective Lokas? What is the symbolic significance of this?

- What is the symbolic representation of the trinity, seeing the whole universe in the toe-nail of Devī?
- What is a Universe?
- What is our role in this Universe?

Have you watched the movie "Inception"? It speaks of dreams within dreams.

Similarly, **we live in a universe that is part of a multiverse**, a universe inside a universe.

So, where am I in this Universe??

I am a minuscule part of this vast universe.

I am like a speck of sand on a beach; nonetheless, every speck of sand helps create the beach. The essence of every spec of sand is the same as the beach.

I am like a drop of water in the ocean; nonetheless, every drop of water helps form the ocean. The essence of every drop is the same as that of the ocean.

I am insignificant and expansive at the same time.

CHAPTER 2

Vasudhaiva Kutumbakam

(THE WORLD IS ONE FAMILY)

If this Universe is like a Super-Organism, what are you in it? A Cell?

If this Universe is my home, who do you think would be your family?

What is your role in this Universe?

How can one be expansive and insignificant at the same time....

Dive into this chapter to know more....

अयं निजः परो वेति गणना लघुचेतसाम्।
उदारचरितानां तु वसुधैव कुटुम्बकम्॥

ayaṃ nijaḥ paro veti gaṇanā laghucetasām
udāracaritānāṃ tu vasudhaiva kuṭumbakam

Only small men discriminate saying: One is a relative; the other is a stranger. For those of big hearts, the whole world is a family".

-Chapter 6, Verse 72 of the Maha Upanishad.

Our lives are dependent on

- air, water, and food that Mother Nature provides.
- farmers who grow our food,
- transportation system that transports the food to us,

- shops and shopkeepers who make the food obtainable to us,
- parents who nourish us, keep us safe and fulfil our needs.
- schools that give us education.
- people who lay the roads.
- people who make the gadgets that we use.
- microbes that keep the soil aerated so that the water can enter the ground and not cause flooding, and many more.... try adding to this list with a silent gratitude to all.

In a human being, we know that the cells of the stomach are dependent on the liver cells, the lungs are dependent on the heart for smooth functioning, and so on. Similarly, all living beings in this world are interdependent on each other.

During the COVID pandemic, all the countries helped each other with oxygen, vaccinations, hospital accessories, etc, like one big family.

So now, let's think....... how big is your family, how big is your home?

Is your home as big as your family?

Is it as big as your society?

Is nature your home?

Or is the world or universe your home?

The bigger the home, the bigger the heart, that includes all, respects all, loves all and is able to co-exist.

Pṛthu Maharaj was a king who thought of the inhabitants of the whole world as his family and served the people with the attitude of serving the Supreme Being.

PṚTHU MAHARAJ

(A STORY FROM THE ŚRĪMAD BHĀGAVATA PURĀṆA)

In the lineage of King Dhruva, was a king named Aṅga. He had a son named Vena who was evil. When Vena grew up and occupied the throne, he turned out to be a very cruel and arrogant ruler. His atrocities increased with each passing day. He tortured his subjects, he never followed any scriptural teachings, and was ruthless in extracting his taxes. He even went to the extent of denying all the devatas and declared that all of the sacrificial offerings should be made to him. Blinded by arrogance, he imagined himself as the Supreme Being of the universe. According to him, there was no God other than himself. The effort of the sages to show him the path of righteousness was in vain. To end the anarchy, the sages cursed the king to death.

However, with the death of King Vena, lawlessness reigned supreme in the kingdom. Bandits looted houses; there was chaos everywhere. Therefore, the sages had to get a new king. It so happened that Vena's mother had preserved his dead body since she couldn't get herself to part with him. The ṛṣis then used a special technology of those days on Vena's dead body and created a new human without the negative traits. The new being was a divine person who was named Pṛthu.

He was anointed as the new king by all the Gods, including Brahma and the seven prominent sages (*Saptarṣi*)). Pṛthu was very pious and, he soon restored Dharma in the society, brought peace and harmony, and ensured that his subjects were treated fairly. Pṛthu was born as a partial avatar of Viṣṇu and was gifted with the power to bring about lasting change. Under the rule of Pṛthu, there was all-round prosperity; even the seas and the mountains made way for his travels out of respect.

When Pṛthu became the king, people didn't have regular food supplies because of the erratic produce from the soil. They complained to Pṛthu about Mother Earth. Pṛthu got angry and he took up his bow and arrow to punish Mother Earth. Mother Earth took the form of a cow and began to run with its tail up. Pṛthu ran behind her and when he threatened to shoot her, Mother Earth explained to Pṛthu, "Before you, all beings on earth lived for themselves. They were greedy and selfish and hoarded everything. There was no one who had a selfless heart, who performed actions for the greater good. Their actions lacked righteousness and surrender to the Supreme Reality. I had to withdraw my bounty to ensure that unrighteous people do not flourish." She begged for forgiveness.

Pṛthu replied that since Mother Earth had sinned by denying food to her children, he would have to kill her. Mother Earth then suggested that if Pṛthu could get her a suitable calf with a pure heart, she would provide her milk in the form of corn for the people. Mother Earth is likened to a cow, who would gladly give plenty of milk when she is approached by her loving calf.

Pṛthu agreed. First, he used his bow and arrow to make all the land uniform so that the milk could flow everywhere. Thus, Pṛthu introduced tilling and agriculture for the first time to the people. Earlier, people lived on fruits, roots and meat. But after Pṛthu's endeavour, agriculture became an established practice among people.

Pṛthu, got Mother Earth tilled, and seeds were sown. Through his tenacious effort, a bountiful harvest was realised by the people for the first time.

What did King Pṛthu identify as his home? Was it his palace, his kingdom or the whole world?

The story shows that if the world is filled with people like Vena, who are selfish and arrogant, Mother Nature does not provide her inhabitants with all that they need.

One righteous man's actions can have a ripple effect. Pṛthu's actions were aimed at the good of all his subjects. He considered the whole earth his home. When people work for the well-being of others, Mother Earth provides all with her bounty.

*In the Purāṇas, the cow is often used as a symbol of Mother Earth. A native cow may not give milk willingly, yet upon seeing its calf, the love in its heart naturally causes the milk to flow. Similarly, the Bhagavad Gītā Dhyāna Śloka describes Lord Kṛṣṇa as the cow, whose heart, filled with love upon seeing His devotee Arjun (the calf), allowed the milk of wisdom, the Bhagavad Gītā, to flow forth.

सर्वोपनिषदो गावो दोग्धा गोपाल नन्दनः ।
पार्थो वत्सः सुधीर्भोक्ता दुग्धं गीतामृतं महत् ॥

sarvo 'panishado gaavo dogdhaa gopaala nandanaha
paartho vatsah sudhir bhoktaa dugdham gitaa 'mrtam mahat

All the Upanishads are like cows; the one who milks them is Kṛṣṇa, the cowherd boy; Arjuna is the calf; and men who are wise and pure, drink the milk, which is the supreme, immortal nectar of the Gītā.

- Gītā Dhyāna Śloka 4.

Journey from "Me" to "We"

Every action of mine has a ripple effect.

If I make "I, me and myself" the centre of my world, my self-centeredness would have a ripple effect on the world around me and in turn, it would affect me.

If I make myself a part of the world, my selflessness will have a ripple effect and serve the world around me and in turn serve me.

WHERE IS MY HOME?

If one uses words like "What about me?", "What can I do for myself?", "This is my Life, my world revolves around 'I, me, and myself'." One's sense of compassion and service is limited to just oneself.

When one's world is the family, the words would be something like "What about my family?", "What can I do for my family?", "This is my family." One's sense of compassion and service is directed towards one's family.

When one's world is the society, the words would be "What about the society?", "What can I do for the society?" One's sense of compassion and service is directed towards a larger entity- the society.

When I identify myself as the Self beyond the mind and body, the whole universe is my home. All inhabitants of the world- animals, birds, humans, plants and everything else, are my family. My compassion and service are for every being of the world.

Let us explore this through a few day-to-day examples:

Example 1:

My house is my home.

Action 1: I like a clean house. I sweep the house and push the dust out onto the street.

Consequence 1: The street becomes dirty. When someone walks through the door, the dust may come right back into the house. I get irritated and wonder why the house is dirty despite having cleaned it.

The society is my home.

Action 2: I want the people in my society to be healthy and would like my society to be clean. I sweep the house and put the dust into a dustbin.

Consequence 2: The house is clean and the society is clean.

Nature is my home.

Action 3: I understand that my life is dependent on the ecosystem in nature. I do not want my waste to endanger living beings. I segregate my dry waste and wet waste. I follow the 3 R's- Reduce, Reuse and Recycle. I live a life of "Less is More." I don't hoard resources because I know, "Earth has enough for man's need but not man's greed". I choose biodegradables over single-use products.

Consequence 3: The air is cleaner, the water is cleaner, and the food that I eat does not have pesticides and toxic residues. I am healthier.

The world is my home.

Action 4: I practice moderation in my consumption. I know that although the money belongs to me, the resources belong to the people of the world. When I buy in excess or waste resources, I know I am depriving someone in the world of their needs. I choose to buy products made or grown locally as much as possible. I minimise wastage. The world is my Home.

Consequence 4: A cleaner world, a bigger family, contentment, connectedness, and simple living.

The Supreme Self is my home.

Action 5: I work towards keeping my thoughts and emotions clean so I can be in touch with the Supreme.

Consequence 5: My needs would be fewer. I buy fewer resources, so there is less to clean or maintain. I feel more peaceful and joyous with whatever I have. I am less fatigued. I feel content and complete.

Example 2: Studying/Working

My Ego is my home.

Action 1: I study/work hard so I can fulfil my desires. I do not have time for my parents or family.

Consequence 1: I get a life that I desire. My wants, which satisfy my ego, are important, and I do not have the time to help my parents or be there for my family. I lose connection with them. I feel alone. They feel alone.

My family is my home.

Action 2: I study/work hard, so I can meet my needs and the needs of my *family*. I spend time with them.

Consequence 2: A happy family and a happy me.

The society is my home.

Action 3: I study/work hard so that I can be a positive contributor to society.

Consequence 3: My family and I are taken care of because we are a part of the society that I serve. My home, the society, is a happy place to live in.

The Supreme Self is my home.

Action 4: I study/work hard so that I can live this life in alignment with the purpose the Universe has designed for me, with a sense of surrender to the Supreme Reality. My every action is an offering to life itself.

Consequence 4: I feel content in life. With fewer expectations, my energy is well-preserved and I can work more. I grow to be a better human being each day, learning from my experiences and others' too. I experience harmony within and around me.

Did you know:

There is no word for "Rights" in Sanskrit.

There is "Duty" - Dharma

The first time, the word "Rights" was introduced to the people of India was through the Urdu word "Haq".

यज्ञार्थात्कर्मणोऽन्यत्र लोकोऽयं कर्मबन्धनः |
तदर्थं कर्म कौन्तेय मुक्तसङ्गः समाचर ||

yajñārthāt karmaṇo 'nyatra loko 'yaṁ karma-bandhanaḥ
tad-arthaṁ karma kaunteya mukta-saṅgaḥ samāchara

Work must be done as a yajna to the Supreme Lord; otherwise, work causes bondage in this material world. Therefore, O son of Kunti, for the satisfaction of God, perform your prescribed duties, without being attached to the results.

- Bhagavad Gītā Chapter 6, Verse 9

CHAPTER 3

The World Is a Dream

Where do I perceive my dreams? In my mind, right?

I also perceive this world in my mind!!!!!

Wondering how? Deep dive into the chapter to know more...

Let me start by asking you a question.

Place a book on top of a table.

Now, if you were asked, "Where do you see the book?"

You would say, "On the table."

If I prodded you further, you might say, "I see the book on a table in the room."

But now, think scientifically and answer the same question - "Where do you see the book?"

The answer lies in your middle school science textbook.

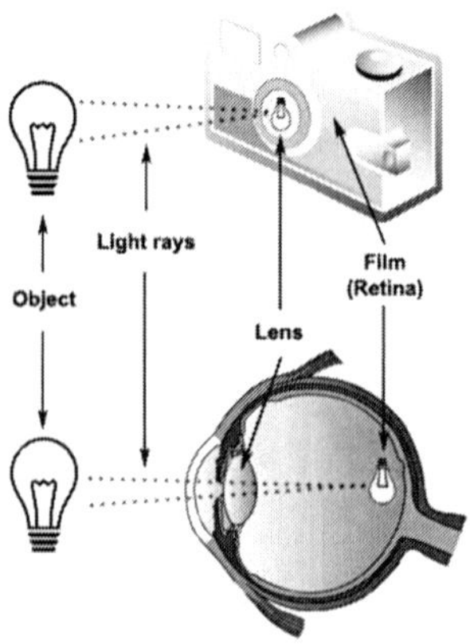

Light falls on an object, passes through the lens and falls on the retina creating an inverted image which is then carried by the optical nerves to the brain, which then projects the straightened image onto the mind screen.

So, what is the answer to the question "Where do you see the book?"

It is "In my mind."

The world I see is an image in my mind. Mind-boggling, isn't it?

Now, the image that humans see is different from the image that snakes see. The difference is shown in the picture below.

Which of these images do you think is the right image of the mouse?

The human image or the snake image or both?

Humans and animals see the image of the world in their minds as per the design of the lenses of their eyes.

This difference in the way we see the world is called perception. What a human and an animal perceive are their own subjective reality.

Reality is something beyond all subjective realities.

What I experience through my senses, is it a perception or reality?

If I look at myself through a concave mirror, I look different. If I look at myself through a convex mirror, I look different. If I look at myself through a flat mirror, I look different. Which of these is real? They are all images as reflected by the mirrors and the lens of my eyes.

So, my perception of the world is based on my eyes, ears, nose, etc., and thereby limited. My perception is not the reality.

Perceptions that are limited by the sense organs are further limited by my mind.

THE ENEMIES OF THE MIND - ARISHADVARGA

त्रिविधं नरकस्येदं द्वारं नाशनमात्मनः |
कामः क्रोधस्तथा लोभस्तस्मादेतत्त्रयं त्यजेत् ||

tri-vidhaṁ narakasyedaṁ dvāraṁ ***nāśhanam ātmanaḥ***
kāmaḥ krodhas tathā lobhas tasmād etat trayaṁ tyajet

There are three gates leading to the hell of self-destruction for the soul-lust, anger, and greed. Therefore, one should abandon all three.

- Bhagavad Gītā Chapter 16 Verse 21

The mind further causes a deflection of reality due to the enemies of the mind, the Ariṣaḍvarga.

KĀMA - CRAVINGS

In the Rāmāyaṇa, Rāvaṇa, the king of Lanka, heard about the beauty of Sītā from his sister Surpanakha. Rāvaṇa had a deep desire to possess the beautiful Sītā even though he knew she was the wedded wife of Lord Rāma. In his deep desire, he kidnapped Sītā. He deluded himself that he was doing the right thing, that a lady as beautiful as Sītā belonged in the palace as his queen and not in some forest with an ascetic king Rāma.

Rāvaṇa's irrational desire became his enemy and led to his downfall. He was killed by Lord Rāma in a war. When desires are held lightly, they do not affect us. But when a **desire becomes an obsession, it leads us away from reality**.

KRODHA - ANGER

Kāma and Krodha usually go together. When a desire is unfulfilled, there is anger. In the Ramayana, Surpanakha, the sister of Rāvaṇa, desired Rāma. But when she approached him, he refused to accept her, as he was already married to Sītā. The enraged Surpanakha tried to attack Sītā. To save Sītā, Lakshmana cut the nose of Surpanakha.

Surpanakha, filled with anger and a feeling of vengeance, approached her brother Rāvaṇa. She described the beauty of Sītā and instigated Rāvaṇa to kidnap her.

Unbridled anger leads to feelings of vengeance and destroys one's Self and the world.

LOBHA - GREED

In the Mahābhārata, Duryodhana wanted the kingdom of Hastināpura for himself. He convinced his father, Dhṛtarāṣṭra, to give an uninhabitable land - Khāṇḍavaprasta to the Pāṇḍavas, so he could rule over Hastināpura. However, when the Pāṇḍavas turned Khāṇḍavaprastha into the beautiful Indraprastha, Duryodhana wanted to have that too for himself.

He invited his cousins, the Pāṇḍavas, to play a game of dice and, through deceit, exiled them to the forests. He then annexed

Indraprastha. Even after the Pāṇḍavas returned from exile, he refused to return Indraprastha. In the negotiation that followed, he refused to give them even 5 villages instead of Indraprastha.

This greed became Duryodhana's enemy and led to the Kurukshetra war, where he and the whole Kuru dynasty were killed.

MOHA - ENTANGLEMENT OR ATTACHMENT

Dhṛtarāṣṭra was deeply attached to his son, Duryodhana. Dhṛtarāṣṭra was blind. He had been denied the throne of Hastināpura because, according to the rules of Hastināpura, a blind person could not be the king. A disappointed Dhṛtarāṣṭra tried to fulfil his desire through his son. He wanted Duryodhana to become the king. Due to this entanglement with his son, he was blind to all the adharmic activities that Duryodhana indulged in.

He felt a weakness towards Duryodhana and instead of showing the right direction to his son, he went along with all his plans to destroy the Pāṇḍavas. This led to the Kurukshetra war, in which all of the hundred Kaurava brothers were killed. **Dhṛtarāṣṭra's attachment to his sons became his enemy** and led to him losing his sons, his peace of mind and happiness.

MADA - ARROGANCE

A group of friends went to eat in a restaurant in a Scandinavian country. They ordered many items. They ate a little and left the rest. The manager asked if they would like to have their food packed. However, the group refused. The manager insisted. The group of friends felt offended and refused to take the leftover food.

The manager called the police. The policeman insisted that they should carry the leftovers with them, else face imprisonment.

The group of friends arrogantly justified themselves , "It is our money. We have bought the food. The food is ours and we can choose to waste it." The policeman replied, "The money may be yours, but the food belongs to the society. You can't waste it. If you had ordered just enough, it could have been used by someone else." The group didn't pay heed to the reasoning in the policeman's statement. They continued to act arrogantly and were jailed.

Arrogance is an enemy of the mind wherein one **considers every situation solely from their point of view and disregards or puts down others' views.**

Mātsarya - Jealousy

In a small village nestled beside a serene lake, lived two young farmers, Raj and Arjun. Raj, a kind and generous soul, was known for his bountiful harvests and his ability to share his produce with everyone in the village. Arjun, on the other hand, was envious of Raj's success. He worked tirelessly, yet his crops were meagre, and he harboured a deep-seated jealousy towards Raj.

One day, a severe drought struck the village, leaving the crops parched and the villagers desperate. Raj, ever compassionate, offered to share his stored grain with those in need. Arjun, however, refused to accept any assistance, instead choosing to watch as his fellow villagers relied on Raj's generosity.

As the drought worsened, Arjun's envy turned into resentment. He accused Raj of using magic in growing and harvesting his crops and blamed him for the villages woes. Their heated argument escalated, and Arjun, fuelled by his envy, accused Raj of stealing his hard-earned crops.

The villagers, witnessing the escalating dispute, intervened, and Raj, despite Arjun's accusations, maintained his composure and spoke about his hard work and the blessings of nature.

The villagers, having witnessed Raj's generosity and kindness throughout the crisis, stood by him. Arjun, exposed by his own jealousy, was ostracised from the village.

Whenever I am disturbed, it is because I am living in a dream world created by my own deluded thoughts influenced by kāma, krodha, lobha, moha, mada, and Mātsarya. We all live in our make-believe world called jagat.

- If I have a deep conditioning to think the world is a bad place, I will see everything that happens as bad.
- If I have had a safe and largely harmonious upbringing, I experience the world as a good place.

THE WORLD IS A MOVIE

We are actors in a movie

The world is a projection on the screen of Consciousness, like the movie being shown on the screen in the theatre.

The movie has a director, actors, a story and a setting.

It is played on the screen in a movie theatre.

Example 1: The "Perfect Life" Movie

Scenario:

You scroll through social media and see someone's picture-perfect vacation.

- **Story writer (Desire)**: *"I wish I had that kind of life."*
- **Characters**: You become the struggler; the other person becomes "lucky" or "privileged."
- **Setting**: Your own room suddenly feels small and dull.
- **Director**: Envy and comparison edit the scenes.
- **Resulting Movie**: The mind plays *"My Life Is Not Enough."*
- **Reality Check**: That photo is one moment, not the full film of their life.

Example 2: The "Unfair Boss" Movie

Scenario:

Your boss gives feedback that your project needs improvement.

- **Story writer (Desire):** *"I want recognition."*
- **Characters:** Boss becomes "critical" or "against me."
- **Setting:** The office feels tense.
- **Director:** Ego and insecurity direct the tone of the story.
- **Resulting Movie:** *"No one sees my effort."*
- **Reality Check:** Maybe the boss was helping you refine your work, not attacking you.

Knowing the difference between stories of the mind and reality is wisdom.

Here is a story of a great mathematician whose mind spun out stories and new actors.

THE BEAUTIFUL MIND

The movie "The Beautiful Mind" is based on the true story of a great mathematician, John Nash, who suffered from schizophrenia. In simple terms, schizophrenia is a mental disorder where people cannot tell what is real and what is not.

John Nash was passionate about mathematics. He thought about mathematics all the time. Because his mind was always preoccupied with numbers, he did not know how to connect with people. This made him feel lonely.

He felt very lonely when he joined college. He had a deep desire for a friend and hence his mind projected two characters- a roommate and his niece. John Nash believed both were real and often had conversations with them.

This went on for many years until one day, his wife realised that he was seeing people in his mind and pointed it out to him.

John Nash refused to believe that the roommate and his niece were not real.

One day, he realised that the niece, the little girl, had never grown over the years.

The fact that the niece remained the same age over many years made him realise that the roommate and the little girl were not real. He realised that they were a figment of his mind's imagination.

Then started his journey from unreality to reality.

Through consistent efforts and guidance from his wife, he stopped reacting to the unreal friends when they tried to talk to him. He saw the two characters, but chose not to respond to them and ignored them. Slowly, the unreal characters lost power over him and stopped disturbing him. John Nash had won over his mind.

What did John Nash do to win over his mind? What makes the unreal lose its power? The answer is to just ignore the overthinking, disturbing mind and know that thoughts are not real and only a perception. Truth is beyond perception.

What we perceive based on the limited senses and mind is only a deflected reality, a virtual reality.

Thinking cap:

Our eyes are like the Virtual Reality glasses that a video gamer wears while playing video game on the screen. Even though the game happens on a 2D screen, he experiences a 3D reality. He experiences himself walking through the roads, fighting with people, jumping over buildings and resting in the game, as though it is a reality.

This world is like the 3D reality we experience through the virtual reality glasses of our eyes. The world we experience is only a game and we are characters in the game.

REALITY BEYOND THE VIRTUAL REALITY!!!!

How can I know the truth from the untruth?

How can I know the difference between the real and the unreal?

The Seers and Sages have sifted the real from the unreal and presented their experience as a path to find the truth, through the scriptures.

The Shanti Mantra from the Brhadaranyaka Upanishad says: -

ॐ असतो मा सद्गमय ।

तमसो मा ज्योतिर्गमय ।

मृत्योर्मा अमृतं गमय ।

ॐ शान्तिः शान्तिः शान्तिः ॥

Oṁ asato mā sadgamaya
tamasomā jyotir gamaya
mrityormāamritam gamaya
Oṁ śhānti śhānti śhāntiḥi

Lead me from the unreal to the real, lead me from darkness to light,

Lead me from death to immortality.

May peace be, may peace be, may peace be.

With careful contemplation on the teachings of the seers (Rishi), we too can see the truth beyond the unreal.

The next chapter will throw some light on how the Rishi knows the difference between distorted and real knowledge.

Time to Dive in and explore the Reality!!!!

CHAPTER 4

Perception to Reality

How do we know the difference between Perception and Reality?

If everything you see, hear, feel and touch is an image in your mind.... a perception, what is the Reality?

What did the Ṛṣis tell us about the world and its creation?

This chapter will break many misconceptions that you believed to be true....

This chapter could change your worldview completely...

Tighten your gears as you dive in to explore the depths that this chapter takes you to.

How does one know of things?

One gains knowledge through evidence (Pramāṇa). There are three ways to acquire knowledge: Pratyakṣa, Anumāna, and **Śabda**. **Śabda** Pramana is considered the path of gaining knowledge.

Let us look at these in detail:

Pratyakṣa pramāṇa - Direct Perception

This is **knowledge gained through direct perception**. As a child, we learn about the world through Pratyaksha Pramana.

- I am introduced to the rainbow and its seven colours. So, when I see the rainbow, I know there are seven colours in it because I can see them.
- A child is introduced to milk. So, the child believes anything that is white and liquid is milk.

❖ I look at the sky and know that the sky is blue in colour.

But as the child grows and gains knowledge, it knows that what we see is not always what it is. Have you heard of the saying **"There is more to it than that meets the eye"?**

❖ In this illusion, we see a set of lines drawn on alternate black and white squares. Can you tell whether these lines are parallel or not?

❖ Answer: All these lines are parallel, though they do not appear to be so.

❖ I see a mirage in a desert and think it is water. But when I get closer, I realise it is only an illusion.

❖ Even though **I see that the sky is blue, I know that it appears so because of the dispersion of light**. The sky has no colour of its own.

❖ **I see only the vibgyor colours of light, but cannot perceive ultraviolet rays and infrared rays**. These we may know, since they are used in our gadgets. What we see is limited.

❖ **I can hear sounds only within a certain range**. Animals can hear subtler sounds.

Our senses have a very limited range of perception. Neither is everything we see the reality, nor can we see everything that is there. Hence, the senses cannot perceive things as they are, i.e., Satya.

The Ṛṣis did not rely on their senses (sight, touch, hearing, smell or taste) to know the REALITY - Satya.

ANUMĀNA PRAMĀṇA – INFERENCE

This is **knowledge gained through inference or speculation**. For example, I see smoke and infer that there must be a fire somewhere. Many scientists use Anumāna as a way to build a theory. Anumāna is also used by doctors as a way of diagnosis based on the symptoms they perceive.

However, **Anumāna can only have some percentage of truth in it**. Sometimes there may be 80 percent Anumāna and 20 percent truth and at other times there may be 80 percent truth and 20 percent Anumāna.

Once, six blind men came across an elephant for the very first time in their lives. After touching certain parts of the elephant, each one of them started describing enthusiastically what they thought the elephant was like.

One man who touched the side of the elephant exclaimed, "It is like a wall!" The second man who touched the tusk said, "O! It is so very round, smooth, and sharp. The elephant is like a spear". The third man who touched the trunk said, "The elephant is like a snake." The fourth man who grasped one of the legs of the elephant felt that the elephant was like a tree. The fifth man touched one of the ears of the elephant and stated that it was like a fan. The sixth man who caught hold of the swinging tail of the elephant commented, "The elephant is like a rope!"

Are the six blind men wrong? No. Yet, none of them is right, because they are stating only one aspect of the truth and not the whole truth. Their perception is limited. They made an Anumāna based on their limited perception. Similarly, we can't see everything, we can't feel everything, we can't experience everything. Therefore, we speculate.

NOT EVERY LIMP NEEDS A DIAGNOSIS

Here is a funny story showing that not all inferences are true. They may be only speculations.

Some of the top doctors from various fields had gathered at a prestigious medical conference. After a long session of discussions and presentations, they stepped out for lunch, enjoying some rare moments of sunshine and small talk.

Just then, across the compound wall, they noticed a man walking by, limping noticeably with each step.

Naturally, their professional instincts kicked in.

The orthopaedic surgeon said confidently, "Looks like a classic case of a slipped disc, probably spinal disc prolapses."

The neurologist shook his head. "No, no. That gait disturbance is more neurological. I'd say, early signs of Alzheimer's, or maybe even Parkinson's."

The rheumatologist chimed in, "Gentlemen, it's clearly arthritis. Look at that uneven stride."

Soon, what began as a casual observation turned into a full-blown debate, complete with arguments, references, and raised voices, each expert determined to prove *their* diagnosis right.

Finally, someone suggested the obvious:

"Why don't we just ask the man?"

They called out to him and asked kindly, "Sir, we noticed you're limping. May we know what's wrong?"

The man looked at them for a moment, confused, then smiled.

"Oh, that? I'm just dragging my feet because my slipper is torn. I'm looking for a cobbler!"

In Anumāna or speculation, reality can get distorted. For example, Satya can get twisted due to gossip where the news strays from reality. Similarly, **overthinking can cause distortion due to Anumāna**.

Anumana is like Chinese whispers? The word that is passed from one player to another gets completely distorted by the time it reaches the last player.

Many theories are based on assumptions.

The Aryan invasion theory, based on language and skin colour, was thought to be true for a long time. But after the archaeological findings of the Indus Valley, and the findings in Keezhadi, Tamil Nadu, the theory of Aryan invasion was questioned.

Anumāna is a good means for exploration, but findings based on it cannot be conclusive.

A conclusion based on Anumāna is like guessing the complete picture of a puzzle with only a few pieces put together.

The Ṛṣis did not rely on the MIND and the INTELLECT to know the REALITY - Satya. They relied on **Śabda Pramāṇa**.

Śabda Pramāṇa

I cannot have a direct perception of everything in the world through the senses.

Can I know about the birth and the childhood playtimes of my parents? I can only imagine, based on the stories they have told me.

My parents, too, cannot have a direct perception of the birth of their parents.

Similarly, one who is born into this creation cannot have a direct perception of the process of creation of the Cosmos itself.

ko addhā veda ka iha prāvochat, kuta ā jātā kuta iyaṁ viśhrushtiḥ

arvāgdevā asya visarjanāya, athā ko veda yata ābabhūva

-Ṛg Veda (10.129.6)[v1]

"Who in the world can know clearly? Who can proclaim from where this

*universe was born? Who can state where this creation has come from? The *devatas came after creation. Therefore, who knows from where the universe arose?"*

*Devatas are demi-gods

न मे विदुः सुरगणाः प्रभवं न महर्षयः |

अहमादिर्हि देवानां महर्षीणां च सर्वशः ||

na me viduḥ sura-gaṇāḥ prabhavaṁ na maharṣhayaḥ

aham ādir hi devānāṁ maharṣhīṇŰṁ cha sarvaśhaḥ

Neither celestial gods nor the great sages know of My origin.
I am the source from which the gods and great seers come,
says Lord Kṛṣṇa.

- Bhagavad Gītā , Chapter 10 Verse 2.

Kṛṣṇa says that the world and the Self cannot be known through direct perception (Pratyakṣa) or inference (Anumāna)

To know the Self, you must go beyond the limited sense instruments and the mind. You can know the Self through **Śabda** Pramāṇa.

For example, Butter cannot be seen in the milk - Butter is not available for Pratyakṣa Pramāṇa.

When someone who has churned out the butter from the milk tells us that there is butter in the milk, it is Śabda Pramāṇa.

If I have never seen butter, I have an Anumāna based on their description of the process involved.

When I follow the process given through Śabda Pramāṇa, because I am intrigued and want to extract the butter and experience the butter in the milk myself, it becomes Pratyakṣa Pramāṇa for me.

Fun Question:

A common man has never seen an atom or an electron or proton or nucleus. He has only read about it in a science book. He believes it is true, as he considers the book, the authority. This is **Śabda** Pramāṇa and he is a 'believer'.

If he attempts to experiment by himself, he would be a seeker. And when he sees the protons, electrons, and neutrons, and has a direct perception of it, he would have Pratyakṣa Pramāṇa. He would be the seer of the electrons.

Are you a seeker or a believer?

Śabda Pramāṇa is the process of acquiring knowledge from the authority. The authority can be a Guru or the scriptures.

Vedānta directs us to the reality about ourselves and the world. **Vedānta is our** Śabda **Pramāṇa.**

Vedānta is the essence of the knowledge of the Vedas and the Upanishads. **The Vedas and the Upanishads written by the Ṛṣis are revelations that they accessed in a deep state of meditation.**

Scientists perform their experiments in a lab.

Similarly, based on the knowledge revealed by the scriptures, seekers experiment in a lab. But the lab is not outside. The lab is their bodies (Pancha Kosha) and their Selves.

Seekers dive deep into themselves through contemplation, and the Truth is revealed to them.

The true Self is not there for our direct perception or Pratyakṣa Pramāṇa initially.

Vedas point us to the Self through statements like **"Tat Tvam Asi", "Prajñānaṃ Brahma".**

This is Śabda **Pramāṇa.**

If one chooses to believe the scriptures and accept them without questioning, they are a believer. Which is fine too!!!

However, Sanatana Dharma nudges the seeker to go beyond belief and know it for themselves.

A Seeker uses the **Śabda** Pramāṇa as a guide and follows the process given in the scriptures or by the guru.

When the seeker seeks with complete conviction and has the same realisation that the Ṛṣis speak about in the scriptures, then the truth becomes Pratyakṣa to the seeker. They become the Seer of the truth.
This is a eureka moment for a true seeker!!!!

Thinking cap:

Newton was sitting under a tree when an apple fell on his head. He contemplated on why the fruit did not float around or stay on the tree. What made it fall down? That is when he discovered gravity.

Until he pointed it out, no one thought about gravity. But, once he pointed it out to us, gravity became real to us. The truth of gravity was always there. Newton just pointed it to us.

The truth of the world and ourselves is also there. The Seers and Sastra just point it to us.

तेषां सततयुक्तानां भजतां प्रीतिपूर्वकम् ।
ददामि बुद्धियोगं तं येन मामुपयान्ति ते || 10||

teṣhāṁ satata-yuktānāṁ bhajatāṁ prīti-pūrvakam
dadāmi buddhi-yogaṁ taṁ yena mām upayānti te

To those whose minds are always united with Me in loving devotion, I give the divine knowledge by which they can be with the Truth.

- Bhagavad Gītā Chapter 10, Verse 10

Having said that, no one can know him, **Śrī** Kṛṣṇa (as the Supreme Reality), now states that some people do know him. Is he contradicting himself? When those who are in complete shraddha turn their intellect towards Him, He reveals the Truth. The Truth is revealed and the situation is shown as-it-is, to those who with faith seek to know It.

What is the truth of this world??? Let us embark on a journey in the next chapter!!!!

CHAPTER 5

Big Bang: A Myth

Was Creation a Big Bang????

Or was it an expansion???

Our Rsis say it is a manifestation!!!

What is manifestation?

How did I manifest? Why am I where I am? ...... (you may want to read that again lol)

How is my world chosen?

Discover yourself and your world as you take a deep dive into this chapter.

KING PARĪKṢIT'S QUESTIONS ON CREATION

King Parīkṣit was the son of Abhimanyu and the grandson of Arjuna. He was a great king, and his rule was equated to the rule of Yudhishtra of the Pāṇḍavas.

One day, he had to go hunting in order to protect his subjects. Tired after the hunt, he entered the ashram of a hermit named Shamika. Shamika was in deep meditation and did not acknowledge the King's presence. A hungry and thirsty Parīkṣit was annoyed by this and placed a dead snake around the ṛṣi's neck. The ṛṣi's son, who happened to see this, cursed that Parīkṣit would die from a snake bite in a week's time.

King Parīkṣit was filled with remorse for his actions and at the same time, grateful for the curse. He felt blessed; unlike most people, he now knew the time of his death and hence could spend the days in hand to connect with the Divine.

He gave up his kingdom and retreated to the banks of the Ganges.

Śuka Muni, the son of Veda Vyāsa, offered to help him through the Shravana (listening) of the **Śrīmad** Bhāgavatam.

Parīkṣit told Śuka **Muni that he would like to know everything from the beginning:**

1. **How did the world come to be?**
2. **What constitutes the world?**
3. **What is perishable and what is not?**

The Ṛṣis never took credit for the wisdom they shared, nor did they patent it, because they were aware that it was all just recycled knowledge. They knew that all knowledge came from the Supreme Consciousness and did not belong to them.

Śuka Muni said, "Lord Nārāyaṇa gave all the knowledge to Brahma, Brahma passed on the knowledge to his son Nārada, Nārada to Vedavyāsa, Vedavyāsa to me, his son Śuka".

Śuka Muni told Parīkṣit how the Universe came to be:

"In the very beginning, He alone existed and within Him existed the subtle bodies of all beings, animate and inanimate, in seed form. He is depicted as lying on Ādiśeṣa (Ādi-beginning, śeṣa-remains; Ādiśeṣa - remains of the beginning denoting that universe is beginningless and endless). His eyes are closed as if in deep meditation, having withdrawn from the activities of creation, preservation, and dissolution. He is in Yoga Nidra, appearing to be asleep.

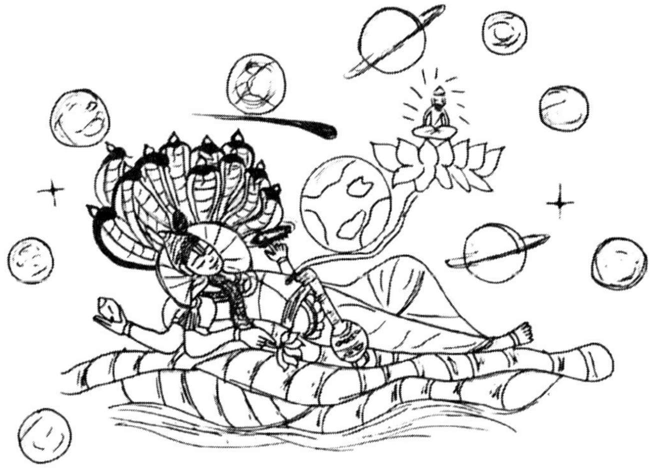

When the time was appropriate, the Lord decided that creation should manifest. From His Prakṛti, five elements sprang out, and there emerged a Golden egg.

The egg split, and out of it came Brahma. (He is called "Swayambhu", meaning self-born). He was endowed with the ability and knowledge to engage in the rest of the creation.

From the first half of the egg, Brahma created the earth.

And from the second, heaven.

Brahma placed the earth in the water and started to create Time, the eight directions, and language. He made the sky, the clouds, thunder, and lightning.

He created the animal world, the human species, the celestial beings, and the sages.

He created the Prajapatis, the lords of the people who could procreate and populate the world. But they wanted to meditate and were not interested in procreating.

However, Lord Brahma insisted and out of respect for their father, the Prajāpati created the devatas and the sages.

The Prajāpati then said "We have helped you, O! Father. Please let us go back to our meditation".

Brahma then created from the two sides of his body, the first humans, Manu and Shatarupa.

He said, "You will live on my earth and so will your descendants."

The descendants of Manu and **Śatarūpā** populate the world.

Over the next few chapters, let us try to delve into the answers for Parīkṣit's questions:

Why are these questions important to us?

Understanding our world helps us understand what we are.

Understanding of our world brings us the freedom to choose "Who I want to be?"

It is by diving into knowledge that the ROOTS MEET THE SKY.

Let's explore Pariksit's first question now - How did the world come to be?

DID CREATION ACTUALLY HAPPEN WITH A BIG BANG??

You must have studied "The Law of Conservation of Matter."

It states that - Matter or Energy cannot be created or destroyed; it can only be transformed from one state to another.

Hence, **there can be no creation; there can only be manifestation.**

What is manifestation?

MANIFESTATION IS LIKE DAY DREAMING TAKING FORM....

Example 1:

- My teacher asks me to write a poem. I write it down on paper.
- Is the poetry my creation or manifestation? Where did the poetry come from? Was it created from scratch?
- There are words in my memory. I use words like sky, water, ocean, etc. that I have heard, seen and visualszed. Did I create the words? Where did the words come from?
- Based on these words and visuals, the poetry comes together in my mind in a subtle form. The poetry is like a dream in my mind. No one else can experience it yet.
- When I put down the poetry on paper or recite it to others, the poetry is manifested. In the manifested form, it is available for all to experience.

Example 2:

- A movie director wants to make a movie.
- He uses a story written by a story-writer. The story-writer picks up incidents he has seen around him as well as his own experiences; he uses the words and visuals in his memory. These become the beginningless causal ingredients for his story.
- Based on all these, an idea comes together in his mind. No one else can see it. When the idea is expressed through writing or story-telling, it is manifested for all to experience.
- The director then visualises the story in his mind. When he makes a movie out of it, the idea becomes manifest.

This universe is the form of the Supreme's daydream!!!!!

The whole world exists as a seed of an idea in the Supreme Being. The universe manifests from this seed of an idea that all of us experience. It also dissolves into the Supreme Being just like a dream dissolves into the dreamer.

HOW DID I MANIFEST?

I was a seed of an idea in the Supreme's dream too. Like all dreams, I too return into the dreamer.

Before conception, I exist as a spiritual seed in the Universe. I choose my parents and am conceived in a spiritual womb, waiting for the right time to be physically conceived.

When I am conceived in the womb of my mother, consciousness enters the single cell or zygote on the first day. There is no body, mind, world, time, and space awareness yet.

My memory from the past forms my predominant personality - a combination of Sattvic, Rājasic or Tamasic guna. I do not engage with the world yet.

After I am born, I am not identified with the body yet, and hence I have no control over my body; I am completely dependent on others for all my bodily activities, such as sleeping, eating, changing diapers/clothes.

Slowly, I get identified with the body. I gain control over the body and start turning over, crawling, walking, running, eating on my own.

I absorb everything that happens around me without any filters.

Since I am repeatedly called by a name, I learn to associate the name with myself.

The world is introduced to me as new food, new things with names, school, my environment, friends, family, etc. A memory of this new world builds in me.

For about two years, I have had no sense of individuality- The "I".

For example, if you ask a child below 2 years whether he took something, he will probably say "NO" while holding it in his hand throughout, not because he wants to lie, but because there is no sense of "I" yet.

Around the age of 2 years, "I" or the ego starts forming. I slowly and steadily have my own emotions, my own thoughts and desires.

Between 16 to 18 years, my Individuality is completely formed. I become an individual ready to explore the world on my own, though I may continue to seek guidance.

I see and experience the world based on the memories I have collected and I continue to collect memories based on how I see and experience the world every day.

Thoughts based on these memories result in desires which in turn manifest as my world.

MANIFESTATION OF COFFEE WORLD THROUGH COFFEE THOUGHTS

Once, a Svāmījī met his student who had studied engineering but was now a successful businessman running a coffee estate.

Svāmījī - *"How did you come to own a coffee estate after studying engineering?"*

Businessman - *"I happened to taste some wonderful coffee once. I was so intrigued by the taste of coffee that I started studying about it. These thoughts brought the desire to travel across the world in order to experience the taste of coffee from different places. The more I learnt about coffee, the more I enjoyed it. I became an expert at identifying different types of coffee. The world started manifesting itself based on my thoughts. Many coffee estates invited me to taste their coffee and review them. Newspapers put up tabloids about me and I became well known in the coffee world. I now own a coffee estate where I grow and provide the world's best coffee."*

Coffee was his passion. His thoughts and actions were all about coffee, and hence he became a part of the coffee world.

Manifestation of healing world through healing thoughts

An ailing man wanted a holistic healing solution for his ailment. He visited a yoga teacher to find a cure for his ailment.

The yoga teacher taught him some pranayama - breathing exercises.

The man practiced his pranayama regularly. Slowly, his ailment got better and soon he was completely cured.

He was so grateful for the change that yoga had brought in his life that he wanted it to benefit and heal many others.

He trained to be a yoga teacher and helped many others to heal.

His gratefulness for his healing made him a part of a world where he could help heal others.

We see many worlds around us, don't we?

The medical world, the space scientist world, the domestic help world.

As our thoughts, so is our world.

There seem to be many worlds in this world. Some people live in poverty and yet seem happy; some are in poverty and miserable. Some others living in palatial buildings are sad, while some are content.

WHAT MAKES MY WORLD

A wise man is sitting under a tree at the entrance to a village. A stranger walks into the village and notices the wise man.

Stranger – "Hello!! I am new to this village. I am looking for employment. I would like to know what this village is like. Are the people warm and friendly or gossiping and hurtful?"

The wise man - "What were the people like in your earlier village?"

Stranger - "Oh, they were very mean and narrow-minded people. They were into gossip and pettiness. I cannot wait to get employed elsewhere and leave the village."

The wise man - "If that is the case, you shouldn't move into this village. The people of this village are the same. You will face the same issues you faced in your earlier village."

Stranger - "Thank you very much. You seem like a wise man. I will take your advice. I would not want the trouble of moving into a village where the people are hurtful."

The stranger leaves. After a few days, another stranger visits the village.

The stranger - "Hello!! I am new to this village. I am looking for employment. I would like to know what this village and its people are like."

The wise man - "What were the people like in your earlier village?"

The stranger - "Oh!! They were ever so lovely. Such warm and friendly people. I would never leave the village if possible. I miss them so much."

The wise man - "I think you should move into this village. The people are the same as in your other village, very warm and friendly."

Why did the wise man say different things to the two people? He knew that our worldview is based on our mind/thought view. If my mind is filled with warm memories, the world seems like a warm place wherever I am. If my mind is filled with hurtful memories, the world seems like a scary place to live in.

Did you know?

We are riding on nearly 40,000 to 60,000 thoughts every day without being aware of them.

उद्धरेदात्मनात्मानं नात्मानमवसादयेत् ।
आत्मैव ह्यात्मनो बन्धुरात्मैव रिपुरात्मनः ॥

uddhared ātmanātmānaṁ **nātmānam avasādayet**
ātmaiva hyātmano bandhur ātmaiva ripur ātmanaḥ

Elevate yourself through awareness, and not degrade yourself, for the mind can be the friend and also the enemy of the self.

- Bhagavad Gītā Chapter 6, Verse 5

I project my mind onto the world. When I am agitated within, I feel others are agitated with me. When I am feeling harmony within, everything around seems harmonious.

CAN I CHOOSE MY WORLD?

Yatha Dṛṣṭi Tatha Sṛṣṭi – As my perception, so is my world.

Your world is a projection of your thoughts. Hence, if you choose your thoughts well, you can choose your world.

Whenever you have complaints, the mind tends to become agitated. There may be thoughts of blaming/accusing others.

Step back and ask yourself, who is experiencing the thoughts?

Where are these thoughts coming from?

Be an Observer of the thoughts.

As an Observer, you have the power to choose your thoughts.

THE OBSERVER IS THE SILENT WITNESS

Who is observing the thoughts of the mind and sensations of the body? - "I", the Self.

When you do yogāsana, you observe the stretch of your body. Who is this Observer? - "I" the Self

When you meditate, you observe the breath. Who is this Observer who observes the breath? - "I" the Self.

"I", the Observer, is untouched by the emotions, thoughts or sensations of the body.

The seat of "I" is in the heart centre.

As an Observer, you know that whatever you perceive is only a projection of your mind and senses, and not the reality.

As an Observer, you can eliminate, substitute and strengthen your thoughts.

> **Eliminate** -Do not encourage thoughts that bring in a sense of lack or make you feel unworthy.

Substitute - Substitute with harmonious thoughts; Know that you are worthy and complete as you are. Choose thoughts of gratitude.

Strengthen- Consciously engage your mind in learning and growing. Engaging in divine thoughts, reading scriptures, and chanting are some ways to strengthen the mind.

The world that we live in can seem like a good place or a bad place based on our thoughts…….

Let us take an example: -

- My friends invite me to a video game – Desire.
- I start playing with them - Action
- Now, the desire grows and I begin to play video games more often for longer durations. I start ignoring my studies – Habit.
- My mother notices that I am spending too much time on the video game and confiscates the game.
- My unfulfilled desire to play the game makes me angry – This memory gets stored as Vāsanā.
- Every time desire comes up, I fight with my mother in anger – Action
- The anger grows and the Vāsanās deepen.
- Due to my anger, my grades get impacted; I feel agitated with my friends in school.
- I feel alone. I think this is because of my mother; she does not allow me to play games.
- I have a strained relationship with my mother.
- My grades are low and my teacher is unhappy with me because of my unhappy mind.
- The world does not seem to be a happy place.

Let us look at an alternate scenario where I act with awareness:

- My friends invite me to play a video game – Desire.
- I start playing with them - Action

- Now, the desire to play video games more often for longer durations grows - Habit
- I become aware and observe the nagging desire within me; I ignore the desire.
- I pick up the book and study instead.
- I have broken the chain of Desire and Action; there is no anger or blame and hence the Vāsanā does not deepen.
- During the exams, I invite my friends to study along with me.
- We play games outdoors during breaks and study when we have to.
- The world seems to be a happy place.

Thinking Cap:

When you say 'I", where do you point to yourself? The head, the legs, the abdomen, or the heart center?

The hand points to the area in the center of the chest, to the right of the physical heart, to say "I". This is my heart center and the center of my Being.

When one's mind resides in their true Selves in the heart center, one is filled with unconditional LOVE and FREEDOM.

हृदयकुहर मध्ये केवलं ब्रह्ममात्रम्।
ह्यमहमिति साक्षद् आत्मरुपेण भाति॥
हृदि विश मनसास्वं चिन्वता मज्जता वा।
पवन चलन रोधाद् आत्मनिष्ठो भव त्वम्॥

hṛdayakuhara madhye kevalaṃ brahmamātram I
hyamahamiti sāṣad ātmarupeṇa bhāti II
hṛdi viśa manasāsvaṃ cinvatā majjatā vā I
pavana calana rodhād ātmaniṣṭho bhava tvam II

In the centre of the heart-cave, Brahman alone shines in the form of the Self as 'I'. Enter into the heart by diving deep, with the mind investigating itself, or with control of the movement of the breath and thus abide in the Self.

- Sri Ramana Gītā Chapter 2, Verse 2

When the mind rests in the Self in the heart center, it removes all delusions and brings awareness to reality.

If the world is a dream, how is it that I see a gross world and gross body that I can feel and touch? How did all this manifest? Get to the root of it in the next few chapters.................

CHAPTER 6

Singularity to Plurality

(PARĪKṢIT'S QUESTION - WHAT CONSTITUTES THE UNIVERSE?)

Ever wondered where this world came from? What is its source?

Where did I come from? What is my source?

How do I get this unique body?

Everything comes from a common source. What is it?

This chapter will take you on a journey from the Singularity to the Unique you!!

ONE TO MANY

Water appears in many forms, from subtle to gross, as water vapour, steam, flowing rivers, still lakes, wavy oceans, ice, clouds, snowflakes, and glaciers.

Similarly, the world is the infinite Supreme Consciousness's many forms.

Every seed of thought manifests as your body and your world.

Dive into the chapter to know how thoughts influence manifestation.

The one seed holds the intelligence of the whole tree.

From the seed is formed both the gross and the subtle:

The roots, shoots, trunk, branches, leaves, and chlorophyll.

The subtle sweetness of the gross fruit, the fragrance of the flowers, the roughness of the bark, the petals so soft, and the many seeds.

The essence for the formation of the whole tree, the roots, shoots, fruits and flowers are in the one seed, the Singularity.

One cell multiplies into many cells to form a human being. The intelligence of a whole human being and its function is present in one cell.

As the cells multiply, some cells come together to form the bones, some the blood cells, some the lungs, some the heart, and so on. While the heart functions through the rhythmic pumping of blood, the stomach performs its function of digestion.

One Person Many Roles

One person plays many roles, such as parent, sibling, child, occupational role (Engineer, doctor, nurse, home maker, lawyer), citizen, and so on.

From One Thought to a World of Experience

Every thought arises from the Self.

One thought results in many experiences that are both subtle and gross.

Hunger manifests as the desire to eat food that, in turn, multiplies into many thoughts, actions and feelings. It manifests as planting, farming, cooking, eating, digestion, likes and dislikes.

FROM INVISIBLE TO VISIBLE - THE SUBTLE BECOMES GROSS

Have you ever noticed how a small idea in your head can turn into something big in the world? Like a thought becoming a painting, a dance move, or even an invention?

This is the journey of the subtle to the gross, from the unseen to the seen.

What's "Subtle" and what's "Gross"?

- Gross = Physical, that which is available to the five senses - visible, touchable.
- Subtle = Invisible, energetic; that which is perceived in the mind, such as thoughts and feelings.

Let's break it down with examples:

- **Physical vs. Smell:** A flower is a gross object, while its fragrance is a subtle aspect.
- **Physical Body vs. Energy:** The physical body is the gross manifestation, while the life force or energy that animates it is a subtle aspect.
- **Thought vs. Action:** A thought is a subtle phenomenon, and the action resulting from that thought is a gross manifestation.

So, what you *can't* see often gives rise to what you *do see*.

They are two Sides of the same reality.

Gross Universe

This is the world around us: the phone, food, friends, trees, traffic, all the stuff we can see, hear, touch, taste, and smell.

Subtle Universe

This is the inner world: your emotions, your thoughts, your dreams and life energy. It is not perceivable by all; it can be perceived by you.

HOW THEY'RE CONNECTED

The subtle and gross are not two separate things; they're like the seed and the tree, or the idea and the invention. The subtle gives birth to the gross.

Think about it:

- Before a song is sung, it's felt.
- Before a painting is drawn, it's imagined.
- Before anything is built, it's thought of.

Fun Question:

There is a forest. There are no living beings in it other than the plant kingdom. The branch of a tall tree breaks and falls to the ground. Will there be any sound?

If yes, what kind of sound would there be?

A "thud" sound? Think again.

Answer: There would be no sound. Let us understand why. Sound exists in its gross form only when there is a living being with functional eardrums in the vicinity. When the branch hits the ground, sound waves are formed. This is the subtle form of sound. When the sound waves hit the eardrum, the auditory nerves carry the signal to the brain and the gross "thud" sound is perceived by the mind.

Since there are no living beings in the forest, there are no eardrums to decipher the subtle sound waves and hence there can be no gross "thud" sound heard.

The sound waves are a subtle form of sound. The sound heard by the ear, "thud", is its gross form.

THE 5 ELEMENTS THAT MADE YOUR BODY

Have you ever wondered *what you're really made of?*

No, not just muscles and bones, but something more. According to ancient Indian wisdom, you and everything around you are made of five powerful elements.

They are:

- Ākāśa - Space
- Vāyu - Air
- Agni - Fire
- Jala - Water
- Pṛthvī - Earth

These aren't just "out there" in nature. They are in you, from your thoughts to your heartbeat to your bones.

Let's take a fun journey to see how the five elements go from invisible and subtle to something visible and solid, such as your body.

FROM ENERGY TO YOU

Just like steam becomes water and then ice, these five elements condense from invisible energy to your physical body.

You were once just subtle energy (Vāsanās, thoughts and intentions), and now, here you are - a walking, talking mixture of space, air, fire, water, and earth!

MINI REFLECTION FOR YOU:

- Ever felt super fiery (angry or focused)? That's your Agni flaring up.
- Felt heavy and lazy? Pṛthvī might be high.
- Restless? Maybe too much Vāyu.

Learning to listen to your body through the 5 elements is like unlocking your personal nature code.

THE FIVE SONS AND THE TEST

A poor but wise man named Ramachari had five well-educated sons: Aatreya, Vyāsa, Daksha, Surya, and Druva. Having become successful in life, they began to lose their humility.

To teach them a lesson, Ramachari asked,

"Which of the five elements is the greatest? Bring me your answer tomorrow."

The next day, each son gave his answer:

Aatreya: "*Earth* is best. It takes all the pain - ploughing, digging, yet always gives. It teaches us patience and unconditional love."

> Vyāsa: "*Air* is pure and non-judgmental. It flows freely and connects everything. It teaches us to remain calm and impartial to all."

Daksha: "*Space* changes colours at sunrise and sunset, yet remains untouched. It shows us how to be still and rooted in our eternal self."

Druva: "*Water* serves everything it touches. It flows around obstacles and merges with the ocean. It teaches us adaptability and surrender."

Ramachari smiled and said,

"All the elements are equally divine. They change forms, but never their nature. Let that be your learning, to stay rooted in your true Self, no matter the role you play."

HOW YOU FORMED FROM THE FIVE ELEMENTS

Have you ever seen water vapor turn into clouds, then rain, and finally become ice?

Let's break it down:

- Water vapor is the lightest, *invisible* form of H2O - subtle.
- That vapor condenses into water, still, flowing - more visible.
- Water condenses further into ice, solid, heavy - completely *gross* (i.e., physical, not ewe!).

Now here's the mind-blowing part:

Just like H_2O goes from subtle to gross, so do you.

THE SPIRITUAL SCIENCE OF YOU

According to Vedānta, you are built from the same five elements - Ākāśa (Space), Vāyu (Air), Agni (Fire), Jala (Water), and Pṛthvī (Earth).

But they don't just *appear* as a human body. There's a journey of condensation, like vapor turning into ice.

Let's see how that works:

Stage 1: Vāsanās - The Invisible Seeds

It all starts with your vāsanās, your deep-rooted tendencies, desires, memories (from this life or even past ones), parental and ancestral patterns. These are like the water vapor, invisible but powerful.

If there are no vāsanās, there's no reason to take birth.

No birth = no body = no death.

Stage 2: Thoughts and Emotions - The Subtle Body

Your vāsanās create thoughts, feelings, and perceptions. This is your subtle body, like water - flowing and changing all the time, but not yet solid.

This includes:

- Your mind and feelings
- Your memories and desires.
- Your sense of "me" and "my world"

Stage 3: Physical Body - The Gross Body

Finally, those subtle thoughts manifest into your physical body - the grossest form of the five elements, just like ice is the solid form of vapor.

Now you have:

- A body made of skin, muscles, bones (Pṛthvī)
- Blood and fluids (Jala)
- Body heat and digestion (Agni)
- Breath and energy (Vāyu)
- Space within and around the organs (**Ākāśa**)

What Makes You Unique?

Even though we all have the same five elements, each of us looks and behaves differently. Why?

We are unique because each of us has unique vāsanās and unique Satva, Rajas, Tamas composition.

Your body, personality, and experiences are shaped by these unique vāsanās.

How can you benefit from this wisdom?

- **Be aware of your thoughts; they're shaping your body and life.**
- **Keep your vāsanās light; be mindful of too much attachment, and emotions such as anger, jealousy.**
- **Connect with your inner space (Ākāśa) to stay calm, accepting, and centered.**

Full Circle: From Ice Back to Vapor

Just like ice melts into water and then becomes vapour again, you too will one day give up your physical body. What remains?

Your vāsanās. They are carried forward as your subtle body into the next life.

Therefore, working on your inner self *now* will help shape not just this life, but the lives to come too.

Thinking Cap:

A child that is adopted starts looking like the adoptive parents over time, although they are not biologically related.

This is because they start sharing the thoughts of their parents.

Indians in India look different from Indians abroad over time, because of the differing climatic conditions as well as the influence of the different thought world.

ONE OBSERVER – MANY FORMS OF THE UNIVERSE

Have you ever noticed how you can watch your thoughts and feelings, like watching a movie?

- You observe the world around you—trees, buildings, phones, animals, friends, games.
- You also observe what happens inside— you feel happy, sad, excited, or bored.
- You even observe your thoughts—like the ones that say, *"I want pizza"* or *"I hope they like me."*

That part of you that's observing is the *Observer*.

That's*You*.

There's just one "You," but you experience so many things.

The One Observer sees the whole Universe.

CONSCIOUSNESS – THE POWER BEHIND IT ALL

अहं सर्वस्य प्रभवो मत्तः सर्वं प्रवर्तते |
इति मत्वा भजन्ते मां बुधा भावसमन्विताः ||

ahaṁ sarvasya prabhavo mattaḥ sarvaṁ pravartate
iti matvā bhajante māṁ budhā bhāva-samanvitāḥ

I am the origin of all creation. Everything proceeds from Me. The wise who know this perfectly worship Me with great faith and devotion.

- Bhagavad Gītā Chapter 10 Verse 8

Just like fans, lights, or fridges have no purpose without electricity,

the Universe, the human body and mind have no purpose without Consciousness.

None of these — body, breath, thoughts, work without the Supreme Consciousness.

It is the One Power behind all experiences. It is what we are, not the body, not the thoughts, but the light that shines behind them to reveal them to us.

WHEN NO ONE IS WATCHING

A man once gathered his three young children together. He gave each one a bag of sweets with a simple instruction: *"My children, go each of you and eat these sweets in a place where no one will see you and then return to me."*

Each of them took their bag of sweets and left. A short while later, all three returned to their father. Seeing two of his children with empty hands, the man asked each of them in turn where they had eaten their sweets.

One of them replied: **"Father! I went and hid in my room,** *where I was all alone and ate my sweets. No one saw me."*

Another replied: *"I climbed up a tree and hid there, all alone amongst its branches, to eat my sweets. No one saw me."*

Then the man turned to his third child. The little child still clutched the bag of sweets in its hands. The father asked why it had returned without eating the sweets as he had instructed.

The little child replied. *"I tried to hide alone in my room, I tried to hide up a tree, but wherever I tried to hide, I could not find any place where I could eat my sweets without being seen; wherever I tried to hide, Bhagwan was always there watching over me."*

Significance of Namaste:

It represents a harmonious blend of physical, mental, and spiritual well-being. The gesture is a recognition that there is a divine spark within every being, and by acknowledging and honouring this divinity in others, we promote a sense of unity and interconnectedness.

"Do not look up to anyone or look down on anybody."

"We are all Divine beings at the core"

THE ONE IN ALL

Lord Gaṇeśa was a very naughty child. He loved to roam around near Mount Kailash along with his friends, and was constantly thinking up new pranks to play.

One day, while he was playing, he saw a cat purring away happily. He caught hold of the cat by its tail for some innocent fun. To tease it further, he started twisting the tail until the cat cried out in pain and forcibly wrenched itself out of his grasp. The cat twirled around in the air and fell with great force upon the ground, injuring itself. Yowling with pain, it ran away to its home in the mountains.

When Gaṇeśa realised that he had hurt the cat and caused it injury, he felt sorry and . As he was on his way home, he suddenly started feeling very hungry.

He rushed into his home and called out to mother Pārvatī, to give him some food. When she came to him with the food, he was shocked to see her covered with dust and bruised all over. She was obviously in pain.

He wondered that his mother, being the mother of this world, was so great that nobody could have the strength to injure her in this way and cause her pain. Realisation dawned suddenly upon him. He understood that if his mother was the mother of all life on the earth, then a part of her also existed in all life. When any part of life was pained or hurt, it obviously brought great discomfort to her also. Her omnipresence in every particle of life was Divine. Hence, the pain of the cat, which he had injured, had to be a part of her pain and suffering too.

Humbly apologising to his mother Pārvatī, he pledged to never cause suffering to any part of life ever again.

The lesson of the interconnectedness of life becomes apparent through this simple tale.

अनेकबाहूदरवक्त्रनेत्रं पश्यामि त्वां सर्वतोऽनन्तरूपम्।
नान्तं न मध्यं न पुनस्तवादिं पश्यामि विश्वेश्वर विश्वरूप॥१६॥

aneka-bāhūdara-vaktra-netraṁ paśyāmi tvāṁ sarvato 'nanta-rūpam
nāntaṁ na madhyaṁ na punas tavādiṁ paśyāmi viśveśvara viśva-rūpa

O Lord of the universe, O universal form, I see You everywhere with infinite forms, with many arms, bellies, mouths, and eyes. I see neither your beginning nor the middle nor the end.

- Bhagavad Gītā Chapter 11 Verse 16

CHAPTER 7

The Universe is Ever Changing

(PARĪKṢIT'S QUESTION - WHAT IS PERISHABLE AND WHAT IS NOT?)

Does a river ever have the same water in it twice?

Is your body the same as it was when you were a child?

Has your taste in food, clothes, or music stayed the same over the years?

What does the thought of changing yourself do to you?

When you have to change houses, school or work, how do you feel?

This chapter will gently nudge you to accept change as you learn to embrace the unchanging reality behind the changing world.

THE HIDDEN SECRET

(A story from the Śiva Purāṇa)

This is the story of Amarnathji. The Amarnath cave is where Lord Śiva is believed to have given the Brahma Vidya to Pārvatī Mātā. Read on to know the story!!!!

Once, Devarṣi Nārada visited Mount Kailash. Lord Śiva was in deep samadhi at that time, and hence Nārada met with Goddess Pārvatī.

Nārada said," I came to enquire about the well-being of all in Kailāśa, O Mother!!"

Pārvatī said, "Everybody is happy and living in wonderful harmony, Nārada. My vahana (vehicle), the lion, is friendly with Īśvara's bull, Nandi. Gaṇeśa's vahana, the mouse, and Shanmuga's vahana, the peacock, are both friendly with the snakes around Īśvara's neck, and thus there is no dearth of love, bliss, and peace among all the family members."

Sage Nārada liked to create conflict and confusion that always led to something good in the end. He asked, "Does Lord Śiva truly love you? I assume there are no secrets between the two of you. Is that right?"

Pārvatī said, "Of course, he loves me. There are no secrets between us. Why do you ask?"

Nārada said, "Lord Śiva wears a garland of skulls around his neck. Do you know whose skulls they are?"

Mātā Pārvatī was unable to answer this. Nārada quietly went away, leaving Pārvatī perturbed that there were secrets between her and Lord Śiva. As soon as Śiva came out of his samadhi, she asked him the secret behind the garland of skulls that he wore.

Śiva said, "These skulls are of yours. After your death from each birth, unable to bear the separation from you, I wore your skull around my neck as a memento!"

Pārvatī was surprised and asked, "How is it that I alone take birth and die each time? How come Īśvara never dies?"

Śiva said, "It is because I know the secret of Amaratwa (immortality), and you do not."

Now Mātā Pārvatī became angrier that there was such a big secret between them. She insisted that Lord Śiva should teach her the secret of immortality (Brahma Vidya).

Īśvara agreed to tell her the story on two conditions. "No one other than you should listen to the secret. As I close my eyes and narrate the story, you should acknowledge me with the sound "Um", so I know that you are listening attentively. The moment you stop acknowledging, I will stop the narration and you shall never again be able to hear the Brahma vidya from me."

Devī Pārvatī agreed to these conditions.

Lord Śiva then shook his Damaru so hard that all the birds and other creatures left the place immediately, all but a little egg which was ready to crack.

As Lord Śiva narrated the story, Devī Pārvatī fell asleep while a little parrot inside the egg broke the shell and hatched out. It listened to the secret of Amaratwa and kept saying "Um" instead of the Devi as it wanted to hear the whole Brahma vidya. When Lord Śiva finished telling the secret of Amaratwa (Brahmavidya) and opened his eyes, he saw that Mata Pārvatī was sleeping.

The little parrot who got the secret of Amaratwa went on to be Śuka Muni (Śuka in Sanskrit means parrot) in his next birth, the son of Veda Vyāsa born with the Brahmavidya.

Goddess Pārvatī continues to go through the cycle of birth and death since she did not receive the secret of immortality (Amaratwa).

Pārvatī denotes the ever-changing Universe and Īśvara denotes the everlasting Existence, Consciousness, and Bliss - The Supreme Reality.

मात्रास्पर्शास्तु कौन्तेय शीतोष्णसुखदु:खदा: |
आगमापायिनोऽनित्यास्तांस्तितिक्षस्व भारत ||

mātrā-sparśhās tu kaunteya śhītoṣhṇa-sukha-duḥkha-dāḥ
āgamāpāyino 'nityās tāns-titikṣhasva bhārata

O son of Kunti, the contact between the senses and the sense objects gives rise to fleeting perceptions of happiness and distress. These are non-permanent and come and go like the winter and summer seasons. One must develop the equanimity to tolerate them without getting disturbed.

- Bhagavad Gītā Chapter 2, Verse 14

ONLY CHANGE IS CONSTANT

- If I like chocolate and I eat 1, I feel joy. I eat 2, I love it. Then I continue to eat 3, 4, 5, 10.... Now, the very chocolate that gave me happiness will bring distress to me.
- The nature of bitter gourd is to be bitter. Some people like it, some people do not like it. The like or dislike for the bitter gourd is within us. Similarly, our likes and dislikes for a person are within us. They just live their nature.
- I may have liked to play with toys when I was little. But the toys may hold no happiness for me as I grow.
- A person who was once young and proud of their youth grows old with wrinkles and other aging factors. To attach our worth to our looks can bring joy in the beginning and distress later.
- I may like a person for certain qualities, but the same qualities can cause misery to me later.
- The body, thoughts and desires are all impermanent.

Our perceptions constantly change. What seems good to one seems bad to another; what I liked once, I may not like anymore.

UNCHANGING OBSERVER VS CHANGING OBSERVED WORLD

Everything that I experience through sight, hearing, touch, taste and smell is the observed world.

The Observer is Awareness/Consciousness.

Let us consider some statements that we speak or think in our daily lives to identify what is impermanent and what is permanent.

- "I am sad"

'Sad' is the experience in the mind and the one who is aware of the sadness is "I". Sadness comes and goes but the "I" is eternal.

- "I am tall"

'Tall' is the characteristic of the body and the one who is aware of the body is "I". The body keeps changing through infancy, childhood, youth, adulthood and old age. But the "I" is constant.

- "I am hot"

I experience the heat of the sun and say "I am hot". 'Hot' is an experience in the body. Experiences of heat and cold come and go based on the weather, but the awareness "I" is ever present.

All experiences of thoughts, feelings, actions, desires, pain, pleasure, sorrow, happiness, likes and dislikes are experiences which come and go.

I am not these experiences. I am the one who is Aware of these experiences: The Supreme Self.

WHO AM I REALLY?

I observe a phone in my hand. Do I identify with the phone as me? When I am aware of a phone, I know it is not me. I do not say "I am the phone."

But I tend to identify with feelings and thoughts as me.

When there is anger, I say "I am angry". Like the phone, the anger is just an experience.

I am not the anger. I am the Observer of these emotions.

Similarly, when I have a cut in the leg, I say "I am in pain".

I am not in pain. The pain is an experience in the body and I am not the body.

I am the one who is aware of the pain in the body.

Shift the attention from the object to the Observer "I".

UNIVERSE IS CYCLIC

Śuka Muni once told this story to Parīkṣit- "After the Universe was manifested, time went on. As the earth aged, each yuga grew worse- crueller, more corrupt.

The first yuga was the Krita yuga or Satya Yuga. Humans, Gods, and beasts lived together in peace and harmony.

Then came the Tretha yuga, when conflicts began to arise between people and with it came violence and sorrow. In this yuga, Viṣṇu came to earth in his incarnations as Parashurama and Rāma.

The third was the Dvāpara yuga. The battles grew fiercer and fiercer, ending in the great war, the Mahābhārata; thousands perished in this war, which was presided over by Viṣṇu, incarnated as Kṛṣṇa.

The last Yuga is the Kali Yuga, a time of sin, corruption, and great destruction.

When the Kali-yuga ends, the earth is cleansed and the Satya-yuga starts again.

This cycle of yugas happens seventy-one times (1 manvantara) after which, Brahma begins pralaya or destruction and destroys all his creations except for heaven, earth, the Gods, the sages, and the Vedas. There is a new Manu as the progenitor of every manvantara.

After fourteen pralayas (1 Kalpa), Brahma goes to sleep and everything he has made dissolves. All creation returns to the eternal ocean from which Brahma and the Universe manifested.

And with this, it is night for Brahma. He sleeps alone in the dark, dreaming of the next day when he will awake and create a new world."

WHAT BREAKS DOWN... GIVES LIFE AGAIN!!!!

Everything in the Universe goes through a cycle of creation, preservation and destruction.

Destruction is very important because it makes way for creation.

Which of these items goes through the natural process of destruction?

1. The man-made synthetic clothes.
2. Plastic
3. Cotton
4. Linen
5. Thermocol
6. Disposables made of leaves

Natural materials go through a natural decomposition process. The microbes in the soil break them down and nourish plants and other living things.

Man-made materials like plastic and synthetic items take much longer to go through the process of degradation and hence cause harm to nature.

To show our respect to Mother Nature, we can choose to pay attention to the method of disposal and the natural process of decomposition of every item, and buy mindfully.

Creation and Destruction are needed for balance in the Universe.

THE HUMAN BODY ALSO CHANGES – CONSTANTLY!!!!

देहिनोऽस्मिन्यथा देहे कौमारं यौवनं जरा |
तथा देहान्तरप्राप्तिर्धीरस्तत्र न मुह्यति ||

dehino 'smin yathā dehe kaumāraṁ yauvanaṁ jarā
tathā dehāntara-prāptir dhīras tatra na muhyati

Just as boyhood, youth and old age are attributed to the soul through this body, even so it attains another body. The wise man does not get deluded about this.

- Bhagavad Gītā Chapter 2 Verse 13

You've already experienced many tiny deaths and rebirths:

- The baby "you" is gone.
- The child "you" has also disappeared.
- Now a teen or adult "you" has emerged.

Each stage ends for the next to begin.

Just like the Universe, you too go through cycles of change from birth to death.

Only the gross body dies at the time of death. The subtle body continues to live and takes on another body for its next life.

When the body is old and weary, the body is shed and the jiva enters a new life and a new world.

WHAT ABOUT YOUR THOUGHTS??

Think about this:

- Are your thoughts permanent?
- What about your likes and dislikes?
- Or your beliefs and even your goals?

They all change, don't they? They rise and fall — just like waves in the ocean.

So, what is unchanging?

THE SUPREME SELF – THE UNPERISHABLE, UNCHANGING CORE

वासांसि जीर्णानि यथा विहाय नवानि गृह्णाति नरोऽपराणि ।
तथा शरीराणि विहाय जीर्णा न्यन्यानि संयाति नवानि देही ॥

vāsānsi jīrṇāni yathā vihāya navāni gṛihṇāti naro 'parāṇi
tathā śharīrāṇi vihāya jīrṇānya nyāni sanyāti navani dehī

As a man sheds worn-out garments, takes on other new ones, likewise, the embodied soul, casts off worn out bodies, enters into others that are new.

- Bhagavad Gītā Chapter 2 Verse 22

At the heart of all beings lies the Supreme Self — the Consciousness that:

- Watches the thoughts,
- Lives through the body's changes,
- and stays untouched, eternal and complete.

This Self is always still, always whole. That is what you are!!!!

FROM FEELING STUCK TO TAKING CHARGE

We feel stuck when we feel "I am the body", "I am the mind".

We feel empowered when we come to know without a doubt that I am NOT the body, I am NOT the mind.

When feeling stuck, ask yourself "Who is stuck?". Seek the true YOU in your heart, beyond the mind and the body, you will feel empowered.

You move from: -

1. **From "Feeling stuck" to "I will figure it out."**
   Example: You failed a test. Instead of saying, "I'm just not smart enough," you think, "Okay, what can I do differently next time?"

2. **From "Going through a rough patch" to "Turning challenges into growth"**
   Example: A friendship ended badly. Instead of dwelling on loss, you reflect on what you learned about trust and boundaries.

3. **From "It is too hard" to "Step by Step I can do this."**
   Example: Too much homework and activities? Rather than panicking, you make a plan and tackle it step by step.

4. **From "No one gets me" to "I can find my people"**
   Example: Feeling left out at school? Instead of sulking, you join a new club or hobby group where like-minded friends hang out.

5. **From "Being held back" to "Choosing my path forward"**
   Example: Parents won't let you take a trip. Instead of sulking, you research safe alternatives or ways to earn their trust.

6. **From "Facing challenges" to "Discovering my resilience"**
   Example: Got rejected from a club or team? Instead of thinking, "I'll never fit in," you try again elsewhere, stronger and wiser.

7. **From "It's unfair" to "I can make it work"**
   Example: Assigned a tough group project with lazy teammates? Instead of complaining, you organise the work and lead by example.

8. **From "Why me?" to "What now?"**
   Example: Lost your phone or something important. Instead of sulking, you figure out next steps calmly and prevent it next time.

FEAR OF CHANGE TO ADVENTURE!!!

Are you someone who is afraid of change? Know that you are not alone.

Fear of change is because I seek happiness in changing objects of the world - status, car, house, job designation, friends, my looks, my intelligence.

When I have to change schools, work, city or country, there is fear of losing friends and familiar space. But if I believe in myself, I will look at it as an adventure and be confident that I will make new friends.

Fear of losing my loved ones- But knowledge brings clarity that everyone who is born has to die one day. Even if one passes away, they live on in my memories.

Even fear of death is fear of change- I think I am the body and hence I am afraid of leaving it. I am afraid of the journey after death, fear of the unknown and I want to hold onto my body. But the truth is, death is only a new beginning. I shed the body to wear a new one.

When I seek happiness in my Self, change becomes an adventure for me.

THIS IS WHAT AN EMPOWERED "ME" WOULD SAY.......

- I am whole. I am complete, just as I am.
- I am ever joyful — not because of what I have or what I do, but because of what I *am*.
- I am eternal. The body may perish, but *I*, the Self, live on, untouched by time.
- I am love. I am compassion. These are not qualities I wear; they are my essence.
- I am charming and magnetic — for I radiate the quiet power of presence.
- No thought, no emotion can stain me. I remain untouched, unshaken, and pure.
- I hold within me the power to release all guilt, all fear, all anger, and every limiting belief.
- I see no enemies. I hold no judgment. I am a friend to all, for I see the Self in all.
- In stillness, I worship Thee; not outside, but within; in the temple of silence.
- I believe in myself. In gain and loss, in victory and defeat, I remain equanimous. I feel Thy energy flow through my hands. Work becomes worship.

When I surrender my mind and body to the Divine with Faith, life becomes a Divine journey.

Lord Krishna says:-

महात्मानस्तु मां पार्थ दैवीं प्रकृतिमाश्रिताः |
भजन्त्यनन्यमनसो ज्ञात्वा भूतादिमव्ययम् || 13||

mahātmānas tu māṁ pārtha daivīṁ prakṛitim āśhritāḥ
bhajantyananya-manaso jñātvā bhūtādim avyayam

The great beings, who take shelter in Me, O Parth, know Me as the origin of all creation. They engage in My devotion with their minds fixed exclusively on Me.

- Bhagavad Gītā Chapter 9 Verse 13

CHAPTER 8

The Parallel Universes

(WHERE ARE YOU?)

When we think of Parallel Universes, we think of universes with many galaxies. But we have already seen that our world is merely a projection of our mind.

Ever wondered? If all of us are born from the same source, why do we experience differences in this world?

When we look around us or read about people in the newspapers or magazines, we find different types of people, don't we? Some who are creative, some who are calm as a saint, some who choose to harm others and so on.

People live within parallel worlds in this one world. The parallel worlds are our mind worlds.

Just like some cells in the body become heart cells, some cells become bones, some blood and some cancer cells, we human beings become part of different worlds based on our mental impressions - Vāsanās.

THE JOURNEY TO MY WORLD?

As a jiva moves from one life to another, the latent impressions - Vāsanā's- are carried over too.

If the jiva has a musical mind and desires to pursue music, the jiva will find a musical world.

Good acts performed will enable the jiva to secure a good life.

If the jiva carries an attachment to a house, person, place, or thing, it will come back to the same place.

If the jiva is filled with anger and vengeance, it will find its place in a house that nurtures anger and vengeance.

Heaven and Hell are not places somewhere outside of us, but worlds in our own minds.

Heaven or Hell is our own making. It is the state of our mind. If my mind is filled with anger, lust, arrogance, greed, and jealousy, I live in hell on earth.

If my mind is filled with love, kindness, servitude, compassion, and joy, I live in heaven on earth.

What you BECOME depends on which mind world you predominantly reside in.

There are 7 levels of heaven and 7 levels of hell as given in the scriptures.

Stories from the Purāṇas often depict the asuras and rakshasas as occupying the lower worlds and the Devas and Ṛṣis living in the higher worlds.

Where are these worlds? Where do they exist?

These worlds are nothing but our mind worlds.

The higher mind worlds or Lokas:-

1. **Satya Loka** - Beings are in oneness with the Supreme consciousness.
2. **Tapa Loka** - Beings of great purity, such as ṛṣis and sages who can easily access the Supreme Consciousness.
3. **Jana Loka** - Beings whose only purpose in life is to serve the world selflessly.
4. **Mahar Loka** - Beings who have achieved higher siddhis or power through great penance.

5. **Swarga Loka** – Creative people such as artists, musicians and dancers (gandharvas, apsaras).
6. **Bhuvar Loka** – Vishwakarma, the engineers who work for the betterment of the world.
7. **Bhu Loka** – This is the plane of reflection and correction; it is the mind world in which beings can reduce their Vāsanās.

The lower mind worlds or Talas:-

1. **Atala** - People who have selfish attitudes; fear and lust are the governing emotions. The enslavement to emotions can be corrected through self-discipline and self-control.
2. **Vitala** -People with higher levels of ignorance; Scientists with negative ambitions, dishonest businessmen, along with people who are either physically or mentally violent, may also belong here.
3. **Sutala** - People with low self-esteem and rigid beliefs and habits. They could also be religious leaders and priests with negative intentions.
4. **Mahatala** - Beings who are very critical and look at the negative in everything; they have very low self-esteem coupled with arrogance.
5. **Rasa Tala** - Tamas of the negative kind is the dominating guṇa of the beings here. There is no self-awareness. There is no attempt at self-reflection.
6. **Tala-Tala** - Darkness prevails in greater measure in the beings here. They know they are wrong and still continue to do it to a greater degree.
7. **Patala** - Beings like terrorists and professional killers who nurture hatred, jealousy, supreme guilt, envy, sorrow, negative attitudes, and have a demonic nature. It is like living in the shadows with the power off. There is no light.

THE MIND IS LIKE A 14 -STOREY BUILDING.

Each storey is a Loka characterised by beings with certain combinations of Sattva, Rajas and Tamo Guṇa. The highest Loka, which is Satya Loka or Brahma Loka, has beings with pure Sattva guṇa. Below that, the Rajas component adds in.

The beings operating in the mind worlds below Bhuloka have lower Sattva, and higher Rajas and Tamo Guṇa.

The Tamo guṇa keeps increasing and the Sattva guṇa keeps reducing with each level downwards until in Patala, there is no Sattva guṇa at all. There is only darkness in such a person's mind.

Where are you? Which Mind World do you belong to?

THE GRAND DESIGN

Nothing is Random

The trees give out oxygen that we breathe. The carbon dioxide that we breathe out is used by trees to photosynthesise.

The food chain, where one living organism depends on another, is not random.

The water cycle, wherein water from the ocean evaporates into water vapour, condenses into clouds and precipitates as rain back into the ocean, is surely not random.

The birds know exactly the kind of nest they have to build - a weaver bird builds the weaver bird nest and a sunbird, a sunbird nest; all these are too intelligent to be random.

There is an intelligence behind this beautiful design.

Which mind world, one is part of, is not a random selection. There is an intelligence behind this complex design of choosing the world, that you would be part of. The intelligence places you in a world based on your vāsanās.

Vāsanās manifest as desires and one chooses where one should be born based on their desires.

If one has gained musical skills in a particular life, and desires to perfect it further, they would choose parents belonging to a world that can help them further their desire in their next life.

If one seeks vengeance for a wrong that was done to them in the previous birth, they choose parents and an environment that will help fulfil their desire in the next birth.

YOU CHOOSE YOUR PARENTS, ENVIRONMENT, and YOUR MIND WORLD, BASED ON YOUR VĀSANĀS.

The Intelligence behind the Grand Design is The Supreme Consciousness!!!!!

CAN ONE ESCAPE FROM THE LOWER MIND WORLDS TO BETTER PLACES?

When one has suffered enough and has built a resolve to change, there is an opportunity to go beyond your guṇa and qualify for the better.

From time to time, Divine beings from higher Lokas take birth to serve the lower Loka entities. They enable a change in their gunas by setting examples, motivating, counselling, and sharing their knowledge.

We have so many gurus who have appeared from the higher lokas, like Ramana Maharishi, Adi Shankaracharya, Sri Raghavendra and many more who have chosen to come to Bhuloka to help spread the wisdom of the Supreme to all.

Surrendering to the Divine intelligence that is behind this creation enables one to transcend their mind world.

Ratnakar who was a bandit, became Valmiki the sage when he met Nārada Muni. He became a transformed person and surrendered to Lord Rama. He went on to write the Rāmāyaṇa, one of the epic scriptures of Bharata.

DIVINE VĀSANĀS TO COUNTER WORLDLY VĀSANĀS

Divine Vāsanās can counter all Vāsanās.

Studying the scriptures, visiting deities in temples, performing puja, chanting, meditating, and listening to talks by great gurus can create divine Vāsanās in the subconscious mind that can counter negative Vāsanās.

When one repents their negative deeds and seeks the grace of the Divine, the Divine Vāsanās within them act as a shield.

VIŚVĀMITRA AND VASHISHTA

Viśvāmitra was not a Ṛṣi by descent and lineage. Before becoming a ṛṣi, he was a great king, a conqueror, and a well-versed scholar who was adept in administration. As a Kshatriya, he was full of valour and ego that led him to victory in various conquests. He was highly Rājasika.

Once, he visited a forest along with his soldiers for his occasional hunting expedition. The team was tired. The King was aware that Sage Vasiṣṭha's ashram was nearby and set out to his hermitage.

Sage Vashishta treated the guests to a rich and scrumptious meal. His cow Nandini, was a wish-fulfilling cow and could give anything that was requested. Vasiṣṭha had arranged a rich feast with the help of Nandini's powers for the king and his men. The soldiers relished the food and were very happy with Ṛṣi Vasiṣṭha. Viśvāmitra, enchanted by the powers of Nandini, had a vicarious desire forming inside him. He thought that Nandini was a cow that needed to be in the court of the King, and not in the ashram of the Ṛṣi where it did not serve much purpose. The king expressed his desire to the Ṛṣi who neither declined nor permitted it. He left the choice to the divine cow. Nandini refused to go with the King. The king was enraged and shot a volley of arrows at Ṛṣi Vasiṣṭha. The ṛṣi deflected the arrows with ease using his Brahma Danda. The king failed miserably. His body and his ego were both hurt, whereas Vashishta was equipoised and left unscathed by Viśvāmitra's humiliating words during the fight.

Viśvāmitra understood that no physical prowess could equal the power of a Sattvic yogi earned through austerities. He decided to practice severe austerity and gain mastery over Vasiṣṭha Ṛṣi.

During the process, Viśvāmitra failed many times.

When Menaka, the apsara, lured him with her beauty, he forgot his tapas due to lust (Kāma). He realised his mistake soon and continued his tapas again.

When Trishanku wanted to go to Swarga Loka with his gross body, Viśvāmitra, out of arrogance, told him that he had all the powers to send him to the heavens. However, the Gods of Swarga Loka said no one could enter Swarga Loka with their physical body and that it was against the laws of nature. Trishanku fell down. Viśvāmitra did not want to accept defeat and hence wasted all his tapas Śakti to create an intermediate Loka for Trishanku called the Trishanku swarga. He lost all his tapas Śakti because of his arrogance (mada).

However, the king soon realised his mistake and didn't give up. Each time, he rose with strengthened determination and continued his austerity.

Gradually, Viśvāmitra gained control over his Kshatriya rājasika instincts and relinquished his ego and anger. He got rid of his revengeful nature and arrogance, attained complete mastery over his mind, and received the status of Brahmarshi.

Vasiṣṭha appreciated Viśvāmitra's efforts and his spiritual achievement.

Viśvāmitra's rājasika guṇa needed persistent and determined effort to gain mastery over the mind and himself.

Choose the DIVINE Over the HIGHER PLANES

आब्रह्मभुवनाल्लोका: पुनरावर्तिनोऽर्जुन |

मामुपेत्य तु कौन्तेय पुनर्जन्म न विद्यते ||

ā-brahma-bhuvanāl lokāḥ punar āvartino 'rjuna

mām upetya tu kaunteya punar janma na vidyate

In all the worlds of this material creation, up to the Brahma loka, you will be subject to rebirth, O Arjun. But on attaining My Abode, O son of Kunti, there is no further rebirth.

- Bhagavad Gītā Chapter 8 Verse 16

All the Lokas and talas are part of the mind worlds. In the mind worlds, we experience the duality of happiness and sadness, pain and pleasure, cravings and aversions. The mind worlds are like a chakravyuha (maze), very easy to get in, but hard to get out. So, beware!!!

Even one in a higher plane may slip down to a lower plane when one fails to recognise the Divine Intelligence behind the grand design because of their ego.

When one surrenders to the Divinity - the Supreme Intelligence behind the Grand Design, one transcends all mind worlds, no matter where they are, and are protected by the Divine.

THE DIVINE PROTECTION

Bali Maharaj, a generous and powerful asura king, was a man of his word. He was the grandson of the asura, Prahalada, the great devotee of Viṣṇu. He, through his valour, conquered all the higher worlds and the lower worlds. He decided to perform a yagna to celebrate this victory.

Lord Nārāyaṇa then appeared in front of Bali Maharaj as Vāmana. Bali Maharaj concurred with Vāman Dev to grant him anything he wished. Vāman Dev asked him for land, measuring his three steps. Bali Maharaj told him to ask for more, as he was the greatest king and owned all the worlds. Do you see the ego in Bali here? To claim that one owns the world, to claim that he is the king of the three worlds, is a show of arrogance. However, Vāman Dev insisted that he wanted only 3 steps of land.

Bali Maharaj's guru Shukracharya, warned Bali that this was Nārāyaṇa himself, come to trick him and take everything from him. Shukracharya advised his disciple to retract his grant to Vāman Dev. However, Bali Maharaj would rather die performing his duty than go back on his words. He offers the three steps of land to Vāman Dev.

Vāman Dev then grew to his infinite size. With one step, he occupied all the higher worlds; with the other step, he occupied all the lower worlds. He then asked Bali Maharaj where he could place his third step. Bali Maharaj realised that the Lord was here to destroy his ego. With great humility, he offered Him his head. Vāman Dev placed his third step on Bali's head to destroy his ego and sent him to Sutala loka, which is one of the lower lokas. However, because Bali Maharaj fearlessly upheld his word and gave his head to the Lord with surrender and humility, He blessed him with His protection always.

This story from the Bhagavad Purāṇa shows that no matter how generous or powerful one is, the ego can pull them down.

Irrespective of the mind world one is in, when one surrenders to the Supreme Consciousness, one is protected.

THE DIVINE'S GRACE IS EQUAL FOR ALL!!!

समोऽहं सर्वभूतेषु न मे द्वेष्योऽस्ति न प्रियः |
ये भजन्ति तु मां भक्त्या मयि ते तेषु चाप्यहम् ||

samo 'haṁ sarva-bhūteṣhu na me dveṣhyo 'sti na priyaḥ
ye bhajanti tu māṁ bhaktyā mayi te teṣhu chāpyaham

I am impartial to all living entities. There is no aversion or craving in me. The devotees who worship Me with love reside in Me and I reside in them.

- Bhagavad Gītā Chapter 9 Verse 18

THE UDDHAVA GĪTā

A Conversation Between Friends

The end of Kṛṣṇa's earthly leela approaches. Uddhava is by his side, as always.

Kṛṣṇa: *"Uddhava, in this life I've granted countless boons... but you, my friend, have never asked for anything. Won't you ask me for something now?"*

Uddhava (smiling gently): *"Kṛṣṇa, I never desired anything, for I already have You. But there is one question that has always lingered in my heart..."*

Kṛṣṇa: "*Ask, dear friend. Just as the world received the Bhagavad Gītā through Arjuna, today it shall receive the Uddhava Gītā through you.*"

Uddhava: "*You guided us to live a life of dharma, detachment, and wisdom. Yet, in the Mahābhārata, your actions often seemed to contradict your words. Why?*"

Kṛṣṇa (smiling): "*Let's begin. What troubles your heart the most?*"

Uddhava: "*You were the Pāṇḍavas' dearest friend and guide. You knew the past, present, and future. Why didn't you stop Yudhishthira from gambling? Why didn't you intervene when he wagered his brothers... or Draupadi? Why wait until the last moment?*"

"*You could have changed the game, tilted the dice, stopped the humiliation. Why didn't you?*"

(His voice trembles, eyes brimming with tears.)

Kṛṣṇa (gently): "*Uddhava, the laws of this world honour viveka—the wisdom to discriminate and act wisely. Duryodhana knew he couldn't win, so he asked Shakuni to play. That's viveka.*"

"*Yudhishthira could've asked me to take his place—but he didn't. Worse, ashamed of what he was doing, he prayed that I not come.*"

Uddhava (shocked): "*He asked you not to come?*"

Kṛṣṇa: "*Yes. And I never impose myself, Uddhava. I stood outside the hall... waiting. No one called me.*"

"*Not even Draupadi......... at first. She argued, pleaded, tried her strength and wisdom. Only when all failed did she let go of her efforts and cry out to me, 'Hari! Kṛṣṇa! Save me!' Only then did I act.*"

Uddhava (softly): "*So... you only come when called?*"

Kṛṣṇa: *"Not out of indifference, but because I honour free will. I am always near, as a witness. But I do not interfere unless invited through surrender."*

Uddhava (with quiet intensity): *"But then, you just stand by while we fall, while adharma wins?"*

Kṛṣṇa: *"No, Uddhava. If one truly knew I was watching, could they act wrongly? You forget I am with you. Always. That forgetfulness is the root of all sin."*

"Yudhishthira erred in thinking he could act outside my sight. Had he remembered me, not just my name, but my presence, the outcome would've changed."

[Uddhava is silent, awestruck. His heart swells with devotion.]

Uddhava: *"So this is the truth... You are the silent witness in all. So, prayer is not a call to someone far, but a remembrance of the One already here."*

Kṛṣṇa (smiling deeply): *"Yes, Uddhava. To realise this is the highest wisdom. I was Arjuna's charioteer, not his sword. I am your friend, but your choice of seeking me or not, is yours alone. Recognise me within and without—as the eternal Sakshi (witness). Merge into that awareness. That is your true Self. Tat Tvam Asi."*

Uddhava (with folded hands): *"I am That."*

The Self shines like the Sun. Its grace is equal for all. If someone does not feel the grace, it is because they have shut their doors and windows to the Self.

One shuts the door to grace because of their ego.

When one does noble work and attributes the result to themselves and their efforts only, without recognising the grace of the Divine Self, that is ego.

Let us explore in the next chapter how one's experience of bondage of the ego can turn to freedom and bliss of the Self.

CHAPTER 9

Empowering Freedom

What does freedom mean to you?

Does it mean doing whatever you want to, speaking whatever you want to, without self-control?

Can we really do whatever we want to, without self-restraint?

Is it freedom to drive on the road without any rules and boundaries? Is this the true meaning of freedom?

Real freedom is when stories in my mind do not mess with my peace.

It's when I can live authentically, without seeking external validation.

Freedom is when external circumstances do not disturb my happiness.

Dive into this chapter to know what freedom truly is.

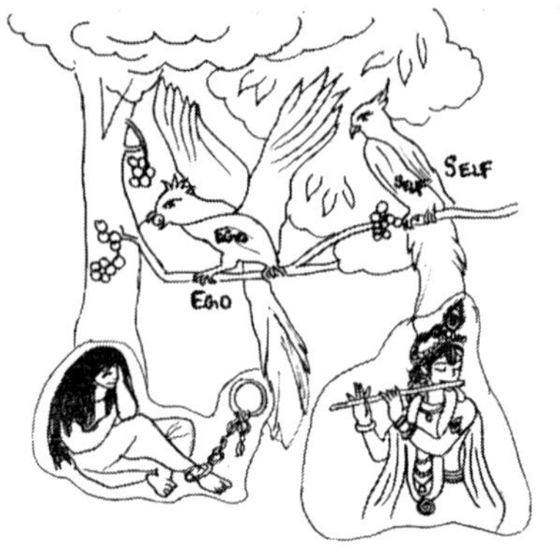

Two birds, inseparable companions, perch on the same tree. One eats the fruit; the other looks on. The first bird is our self that is caught with the mind and body (the ego), feeding on the pleasures and pains of this world; the other is the Supreme Consciousness, silently witnessing all.

ममैवांशो जीवलोके जीवभूत: सनातन: |
मन:षष्ठानीन्द्रियाणि प्रकृतिस्थानि कर्षति ||

mamaivānśho jīva-loke jīva-bhūtaḥ sanātanaḥ
manaḥ-ṣhaṣhṭhānīndriyāṇi prakṛiti-sthāni karṣhati

The embodied souls in this material world are My eternal fragmental parts. But bound by material nature, they are struggling with the six senses including the mind.

- Bhagavad Gītā Chapter 15 Verse 7

THE IMAGINARY BONDAGE OF THE EGO

The ego is me being shackled by the stories and movies of my mind. What are some of these imaginary shackles?

We feel shackled by the people around us.

We feel shackled by responsibilities.

We feel shackled by our own desires and expectations.

We feel shackled by our own fears.

Are we really shackled by things around us or are the shackles more in our minds?

Here comes a story to answer this question.

The donkey that did not know freedom

A washerman visited a village like he did every day. He went to every house in the town, collected all the dirty clothes, loaded them up on his donkey, and set off to the river. After reaching the river, he gasped in horror; he had forgotten the rope at home. He panicked and looked in all directions for some help. Without his rope, he could not tie his donkey to a tree. If the donkey was not secured, it could walk away and he would lose his livelihood. If he went back to the village for the rope, he would not have enough time to wash the clothes. He would lose his day's work, which meant he would not earn money to feed the family.

He was sweating with anxiety when a wise man walked up to him and asked him about his troubles. After listening to his story, the wise man smiled and offered the washerman a suggestion.

"Pretend to tie the donkey with a rope and go to the river. The donkey will graze and wait for you here." The washerman was astounded, but because he lacked other options, he tried it out. He took an imaginary rope, wound it around the donkey's neck, and pretended to tie it to a tree.

He walked a few steps and saw that the donkey had begun grazing. He walked all the way to the river, and the donkey had not moved. The washerman spent all day washing his clothes peacefully, dried the clothes, and loaded them back on the donkey. He patted the donkey, signalling it to move, but the donkey did not move. The washerman was puzzled. The wise man appeared and reminded the washerman to untie the donkey. The washerman untied the imaginary rope, and the donkey started trotting off to the village.

A donkey that is free all the time thinks that it's tied. Similarly, as the Consciousness which is our core, we are free beings. But we dwell in our mind (thoughts) and body and hence feel shackled.

What are some of these imaginary ropes that tie us......

- **Anxiety about the future**
  For example: worrying so much about what career path to choose after school that I lose the joy of learning today. The future becomes a heavyweight instead of a horizon of possibilities.

- **Our never-ending desires**
  For instance: I buy a new phone and feel happy for a while, but soon I want the latest model again. Desire keeps pulling me down without letting me rest in contentment.
- **Our memories of pain and pleasure from the past**
  Maybe I still feel hurt because of a fight with a close friend, or I keep replaying the "fun day" when everything went perfectly. Living in those past moments stops me from experiencing the present fully.
- **Our expectations from ourselves and from people around us**
  For example: I expect to always score top marks, or I expect my friend to always agree with me, or I expect things to work out just the way I wanted them to. When those expectations are not met, I feel disappointed or angry, forgetting that life is bigger than my idea of how it "should" be.
- **What others think of us**
  For example: staying silent in class even though I know the answer, just to avoid judgment. In worrying about what others would think about me, I lose my own voice.

We hold onto these imaginary ropes and sometimes even enjoy the pain that comes with holding on.

We do not want to let them go because it becomes our comfort zone. It seems easier to blame the world, than to face the imaginary rope and change myself. We want to have the cake in hand and eat it too.

A MONKEY AND A BANANA

A monkey saw a banana in a glass jar and desired to have it. He put his hands inside to get the banana. However, the banana was bigger than the mouth of the jar and wouldn't come out. The landlord saw the monkey and came at it with a stick to chase him away.

The monkey struggled to pull the banana out. He looked at the landlord and the banana. He was filled with fear and anxiety, but wouldn't let go of the desire for the banana.

All he had to do was, let go of the banana. The monkey suffered, not because of his desire for the banana, but because he held onto it even when he had to let go.

Like the monkey holding onto the banana, **what are the desires we are holding onto, the stories that are causing distress in my life?**

Here is a Happiness quotient given by Swami Chinmayanandaji: -

Happiness Quotient = Desires fulfilled/ Desires entertained.

When the denominator is low, the quotient is high!! When fewer desires are entertained and we flow with life, we experience Freedom and Happiness.

TO LET GO IS FREEDOM

The Fish that soared high

Some fishes lived happily in a stream. One day the stream changed its course and started flowing in the opposite direction. The fishes were flustered. They did not know what to do. They got scraped by sharp rocks and thorny plants. When they found some softer rocks and plants they held onto them. The fishes started talking among themselves about how happy and free they had been earlier. Clinging onto the same stones for long, they started bickering for space. They felt stuck, complained, held grudges against others, and lost their peace of mind.

One fish looked around at the bickering and complaints and wished he could be free again. He decided to let go of the stone he was holding onto. As he started floating, he was scratched by the stones and plants. The fish then became absolutely alert and learnt to move around the stones and plants. As he found his rhythm with the water, he started floating higher. Now he was able to observe the stones, plants and other fishes holding on to them from a higher level. As he rose higher, he found that the hurdles were lesser, and even when hurdles appeared, he was quick to find his rhythm again.

The other fishes looked at him floating above and thought that he was a special fish, blessed with special abilities. But all that the special fish did was LET GO of that which was holding it back.

When we LET GO of the stories - the desires, memories, attachments and fear of change that is holding us back, we experience Freedom.

I feel self-empowered and complete when I do not give reality to the stories that play in my mind, when these stories do not define me.

HOW TO LET GO??

Know that the shackles are in the mind and I am NOT the mind.

As these shackling thoughts or emotions arise, remind yourself, **"I am enough as I am."** (refer to the section in Chapter 7- "I AM EMPOWERED").

The Observer beyond the mind and body is always free.

As an Observer, I have the freedom to let go and re-write stories that shackle me:

- ❖ "What if I fail?" to "Let me try and learn." - Courage is not the absence of fear; it is to keep walking, in spite of the fear.

- "I always mess up" to "It's ok to be imperfect. Everyone learns by messing up sometimes. I will keep trying to do my best." - Confidence is built like muscle.
- "What do others think of me." to "What do I think of me?" - Believing in the self goes beyond likes and praises from others.
- "No one understands me." to "Let me reach out to one safe person."

The safest being to turn to, is the Divine Being who resides in your own heart as the Self. Close your eyes, feel the presence in your heart and tell your stories and you will be guided to re-write them.

The Power of Now is Freedom

Memories of the past are imaginary shackles of the mind. Whatever incident occurred, it is now in the past.

Every time I recall a memory (good or bad) and relive it, I stay stuck in the past and lose my freedom. In the Now, this moment, we are in touch with the Self and experience freedom.

The Monk's burden

A monk and his master walked by a lake. They saw a lady drowning in the water, calling out for help. The student was perplexed and wasn't sure what he should do. As a monk himself, he had to follow the conduct "Monks do not lay eyes on a woman". However, the master immediately jumped into the water and carried the lady to the shore. He made sure she was alright, and then continued to walk towards the monastery.

The monk was exasperated. Throughout the journey, his mind was filled with the image of the master carrying the lady to the shore. Many questions came to his mind, like "Is this allowed in monkhood? Maybe I too could have saved her."

When they reached the monastery, the monk couldn't stop himself from asking the master, "Master, as per the rules of monkhood, we are not allowed to lay eyes on a woman, but you carried her. Isn't this against the rules of monkhood?"

The master said "I did my duty and saved her. I carried her and dropped her on the shore. But you seem to be still carrying her (in your mind)."

We feel shackled because we carry the past with us. Just drop it.

वेदाहं समतीतानि वर्तमानानि चार्जुन ।
भविष्याणि च भूतानि मां तु वेद न कश्चन ॥

vedāhaṁ samatītāni vartamānāni chārjuna
bhaviṣhyāṇi cha bhūtāni māṁ tu veda na kaśhchana

O Arjun, I know of past, present, and future, and I also know all living beings; but Me no one knows.

- Bhagavad Gītā Chapter 7 Verse 26

"Yesterday was history, Tomorrow is a mystery, Today is a gift; it is called Present" - *Kungfu Panda*

YESTERDAY WAS HISTORY

We carry our memories way beyond their time.

When something hurtful happened to me, it happened to me once. But every time I relive the situation, think about it, or speak about it, I am responsible for hurting myself again and again.

The memories are our shackles.

The memories come up in our minds in the form of pictures or words.

TOMORROW IS MYSTERY

Daydreaming or feeling anxious about the future are both dreams. Dreams are not real.

"Worrying about all the negative things that can happen in the future, is like praying for it to happen". The more I worry, the more I attract worrisome situations. As I think, so is my world.

BEING PRESENT IS FREEDOM

Past and Future are also perceptions of the mind or subjective realities.

Imagine this: There is a 10-storey building with a long road in front of it. There is a person standing on the tenth-floor balcony and another one on the first-floor balcony. When a car enters from the right end of the road, the person on the tenth floor will see it first. What is "present" for the person on the tenth floor is "future" for the one on the first floor, as he will see the car later.

An insect's lifetime is a day for Humans. When it is summer in the northern hemisphere it is winter in the southern hemisphere. When it is day for some, it is night for someone else on the other side of the world.

Hence, time is also a perception of the mind depending on where one is.

The past and future have no existence of their own. I see them in the mind, in the present. The past and future arise in the Now.

Only PRESENT is real. In the Here and Now, we experience freedom.

- ❖ When your mind is filled with thoughts about the past or the future, Observe the breath to be present in the Here and Now.
- ❖ Keep your mind on whatever you are doing.
- ❖ If you are chopping vegetables, keep your mind on that.
- ❖ If you are bathing or eating, keep your mind on that. Be aware of the sensations on your skin and tongue.
- ❖ Practise gratitude for what is, instead of focusing on what could be.
- ❖ Being a neutral observer brings us to the 'Here and Now'.

ACCEPTANCE LEADS TO FREEDOM

True freedom is not about getting everything we want, but about being at peace with what is. Acceptance opens the door to that freedom.

Whenever we give in to the distortions of the mind and act on them, we accumulate karma. The life that we live is chosen based on our Prarabdha karma.

Prarabdha karma is that portion of past life's accumulated karma that is chosen to be experienced in the present lifetime, influencing our circumstances, body and experiences.

It is life's way of giving an opportunity to let go of that which is holding me back. The people and situations are chosen accordingly.

The person or situation that causes the most disturbance is, in fact, life's way of helping me become free from a shackle I am holding onto strongly.

Our parents, siblings, spouse, children and others who we come across are chosen to help us let go of that which is shackling us.

Everything that happened in the past happened just the way it had to.

Everything that is happening now is happening as it should.

Everything that will happen in the future will happen as it should.

Every person in my life is here based on a Divine plan.

The journey to freedom is empowering as I move from: -

Complaints → Endurance → Acceptance → Appreciation → Compassion

AN ENLIGHTENING JOURNEY

This is a story from the life of my guru, Raghuramji. During his younger days, he travelled regularly by bus to Prashanthi ashram wearing a white shirt and pants, crisply pressed. Since he boarded the bus at the starting point, there was a particular seat he always occupied. After a few stops, a vegetable seller would board the bus and always sit next to him. The vegetable vendor, on his way back from the market, would be sweaty and smelly. This caused a lot of discomfort in Raghuramji's mind and the journey seemed longer than it really was.

This happened repeatedly. Soon enough, Raghuramji started experiencing agitation every time the vendor's stop neared, anticipating that the vendor would get in and sit next to him. All he could think of was the smell of sweat and his own clothes getting dirty.

One day, he became aware of his agitation and decided to take control. He decided to **ENDURE** it and **not let COMPLAINTS rule his mind**. Soon enough, he felt, now that he was anyway sitting with the vendor, he may as well converse with the vendor (**ACCEPTANCE** of the situation). The vendor shared his life story and his struggles. The vendor had to wake up early in the morning to go to the market and pick up the vegetables. He then spent the rest of the day selling all the vegetables. He would take the money and buy some ration for his house and return home only to start the whole thing the next day again. Raghuramji developed **APPRECIATION** for the hard work that the vendor had to do and his sweat and dirty clothes seemed less of a problem. He in fact, offered his bottle of water to the vendor knowing he must be tired (**COMPASSION**)

Raghuramji's newfound respect for the hardworking vendor made the one-hour journey seem to pass quickly.

Raghuramji's journey from complaints to compassion shows us that life feels lighter, smoother and happier when we stop trying to control situations and accept them with faith in the Divine's plan.

- **I am free and accept every situation without complaints.** *For example: if it rains on the day of a much-awaited cricket match, instead of grumbling all day, I can choose to enjoy the cool weather, play an indoor game, make bajjis and eat or simply rest. Complaining ties me down, but acceptance sets me free.*

- **I accept myself as I am, and I accept others as they are.** *For instance: I may wish I were taller, or that my friend was more punctual. But when I accept my own body and personality, and when I stop trying to "fix" myself or others, I find peace. True acceptance brings harmony in relationships and confidence in myself.*

- **I accept all situations and consequences gracefully,** without feeling the need to choose or change them. This is supreme freedom.
  For example: Suppose I worked very hard for an exam but still didn't score as high as I hoped. Instead of feeling crushed, I can accept the result as one step in my journey, learn from it, and move on. Acceptance allows me to keep growing without being chained to disappointment.

"Acceptance is not weakness—it is strength. For only a free heart can flow with life, just as a river flows freely by embracing every bend in its path."

Parīkṣit had no complaints when he was cursed to die. Let us understand acceptance through his story.

PARĪKṢIT'S REMORSE

We saw the story of Parīkṣit in Chapter 4. Parīkṣit was a great king. However, when he put the snake around the neck of the meditating sage Shamika, he acted out of character. Every action is followed by a reaction, and hence, he was cursed to die in seven days by Śṛṅgī, the son of Shamika.

As the king had walked away soon after, he was clueless about the curse. Upon reaching the palace, he felt remorseful for the action that he had performed in a weak moment. Then, a disciple of sage Shamika came and informed King Parīkṣit about the curse.

King Parīkṣit, in his heart, thanked the Lord for relieving him of his regret and guilt. He graciously accepted the curse as a blessing. He said, "Most people would not know the time of their death, but I have this knowledge. It is indeed a blessing, since I can now spend the rest of my days with my mind on Bhagwan."

He handed over his kingdom to his son Janamejaya and went to the banks of Gaṅga. There, Śuka Muni, the son of Veda Vyāsa helped him keep his mind on the Supreme, through the shravana (listening) of the Śrīmad Bhāgavatam.

The king died after seven days with his mind on Bhagwan.

When one accepts any situation with grace and surrender, even a crisis can become an aid for transformation. Parīkṣit is remembered even today because of his sensibility, which guided him to accept the situation and look at it as a blessing.

FAITH/SHRADDHA IN THE DIVINE SELF LEADS TO FREEDOM

अनन्यचेताः सततं यो मां स्मरति नित्यशः |
तस्याहं सुलभः पार्थ नित्ययुक्तस्य योगिनः ||

ananya-chetāḥ satataṁ yo māṁ smarati nityaśhaḥ
tasyāhaṁ sulabhaḥ pārtha nitya-yuktasya yoginaḥ

Those who remember Me constantly, I (who is ever free) am easy to obtain because of his constant absorption in the Oneness.

- Bhagavad Gītā Chapter 8 Verse 14

The results of actions are not completely in my hands.

We often think, "*I did this.*" "*I made it happen.*"

But is that the whole truth?

In every action, there are two players at work:

1. **Vyashti – *The individual* (That's me!)**
2. **Samashti – *The collective or cosmic force* (That's the Universe!)**

Let's break it down with a few simple examples:-

Breathing:

I say, "*I'm breathing,*" but what am I really doing?

Inhaling and exhaling - that's *my effort* (Vyashti).

But...

- I didn't create the oxygen.
- I didn't send it to every cell.
- I didn't grow the trees that made the oxygen.

That's all, Samashti - nature and the universe doing its job.

I put food in my mouth and chew it - Vyashti.

But after that?

Digestion, absorption of nutrients, and elimination?

That's Samashti again. I'm not sitting there controlling my stomach!

And how did the food even get here?

Sunlight, rain, soil, farmers, trucks, shops — all Samashti.

Seeing:

I can choose *what* to look at or close my eyes — Vyashti.

But the magic of light entering the eye, hitting the retina, and converting into signals that go to the brain?

That's way beyond my control. That's Samashti.

Moving a Finger:

I decide to lift my finger - That's Vyushti.

But can I really move it just by wanting to?

Nerves, brain signals, muscles, all need to work together.

And if something's wrong with the body, I might not be able to move it even if I try. -That's Samashti.

Cooking Food:

I cook a meal. I chop, stir, taste - Vyashti.

But where did the rice, vegetables, and spices come from?

❖ Plants grew the food, thanks to soil, sun, water.

- ❖ Farmers harvested them.
- ❖ Trucks brought them.
- ❖ Shops stocked them.

And the fire, water, and gas I use? Samashti again.

What's the Takeaway?

Even when I say *"I did this"*, my role is just a small drop in the ocean.

The rest the unseen support system is Samashti at work.

When I understand this:

- I stop being arrogant about success.
- I don't blame myself harshly for failure.
- I feel grateful for everything and everyone that supports me.

The Supreme is like our parent. He knows what is right for us. Everything that happened, everything that is happening, and everything that will happen is his grace in my life and I accept them with all my heart.

Perform your duties with sincerity and dedication as an offering to the Supreme. He will give you what is best for you.

"Effort is mine, Result is His"

In Shraddha "As you walk, the path will unfold"

THE SELFLESS BIRD

A bird and a tree were once friends. The bird made a nest on the tree to lay its eggs, and the tree was happy to have company.

Even after the eggs hatched and the little ones had flown off, the bird continued to visit the tree and perch on its branch. There was unconditional love between the tree and the bird.

One day, there was a forest fire. The little bird saw the tree catching fire and wanted to help. It flew through the flames of the forest to a lake nearby and scooped up some water in its beak to put out the flames. The tree asked the bird to save itself. But the bird didn't stop. It continued to bring water in its beak to save the tree, even though its wings were burnt.

The clouds and the sun told the bird to stop, saying, "What difference will the water from your tiny beak make, in putting out the flames of the forest?" But the bird continued. All it knew was that it had to do something to save its friend.

The clouds were moved by the selfless action of the bird and started pouring down rain. The forest fire was put out.

When the intent is pure and humble, the effort is selfless and sincere, the universe comes together to make the intent a reality.

सुखदु:खे समे कृत्वा लाभालाभौ जयाजयौ |
ततो युद्धाय युज्यस्व नैवं पापमवाप्स्यसि || 38||

sukha-duḥkhe same kṛitvā lābhālābhau jayājayau
tato yuddhāya yujyasva naivaṁ pāpam avāpsyasi

Fight for the sake of duty, treating alike happiness and distress, loss and gain, victory and defeat. Fulfilling your responsibility in this way, you will never incur sin.

- Bhagavad Gītā Chapter 2 Verse 38

The world is a stage

Once, an actor performed his role as Ravana during Ram Leela. He was so convincing, that a person from the audience threw a slipper at him.

The person from the audience later apologized to the actor and said that he got so absorbed with the play and was overcome with emotions. The actor requested to keep the slipper saying, this was the biggest award he had received for his acting and he would like to treasure it.

An actor performs his role with dedication but never thinks he is the role. The moment he is out of stage, he becomes himself.

Freedom is when we perform our roles in the world with sincerity as a student, son/daughter, mother/father, spouse, sibling, friend, and employee, but never forgetting that "I am the Self", and not that role I play.

WHEN I'M TRULY FREE AND SELF-EMPOWERED,

I'M NOT CHASING LIKES OR VALIDATION.

I DON'T NEED PEOPLE TO GET ME OR PRAISE ME

I AM JUST CONTENT WITH WHO I AM.

I FEEL FREE TO JUST BE.

असक्तबुद्धिः सर्वत्र जितात्मा विगतस्पृहः |
नैष्कर्म्यसिद्धिं परमां सन्न्यासेनाधिगच्छति ||

asakta-buddhiḥ sarvatra jitātmā vigata-spṛihaḥ
naṣhkarmya-siddhiṁ paramāṁ sannyāsenādhigachchhati

Those whose intellect is unattached everywhere, who have mastered the mind, and are free from desires by the practice of renunciation, attain the highest perfection of freedom from action.

– **Bhagavad Gita Chapter 18 Verse 4**

SELF-PRACTICE

We can practise every morning and evening for 10 minutes to Just Be with the Self.

Practise 1:

Choose a busy time of the day and just observe the happenings around. Observe the thoughts and feelings arising and settling. Try to hold yourself back from acting or overthinking. Just Be.

Practise 2:

Sit still for 30 minutes with your eyes closed.

- Scan every inch of your body from head to toe, then toe to head, with your awareness. Repeat this for 10 minutes.
- Observe the sensations of your body. Do not allow yourself to like or dislike any sensation.
- When we try to meditate, the mind may say, I had this wonderful experience during meditation last time. I hope I have the same this time.
- Or it may say, I can never meditate. I am always disturbed by so many thoughts.

- These are also stories of the mind. Ignore these and continue to meditate.
- Experience the freedom of not reacting to the sensations of the body and the stories of the mind.

CHAPTER 10

Pralaya-Dissolution

FREEDOM IN SILENCE

The infinite world appears from the Silence; that is Creation.

The world dissolves into Silence; that is Dissolution.

The Self shines through the infiniteness of the world as well as in the nothingness of the silence.

We experience dreams in our minds when our eyes are closed.

We experience the world in our minds when we are awake.

Where does the dream go after the dream state? It dies into the Self.

In the deep sleep state, we experience silence.

When the mental chatter stops, there is silence. The mind dies into the silence.

Silence is where the mind and world rests; hence the term "Rest in peace".

In silence, only the Observer, i.e., Consciousness exists.

गतिर्भर्ता प्रभुः साक्षी निवासः शरणं सुहृत् |
प्रभवः प्रलयः स्थानं निधानं बीजमव्ययम् ||

gatir bhartā prabhuḥ sākṣhī nivāsaḥ śharaṇaṁ suhṛit
prabhavaḥ pralayaḥ sthānaṁ nidhānaṁ bījam avyayam

I am the Supreme Goal of all living beings, and I am also their Sustainer, Master, Witness, Abode, Shelter, and Friend. I am the Origin, End, and Resting Place of creation; I am the Repository and Eternal Seed.

- Bhagavad Gītā Chapter 9 Verse 18

SATYAVRATA

Manu Satyavrata ruled the world in the Seventh Manvantara. Seeing the rising influence of the evil Asuras, he yearned in anguish for pralaya. Lord Brahma too had a cause to hasten the dissolution. He had yawned and due to that, the Vedas fell out of his mouth. It must be remembered that Brahma is not only the creator of the universe, but the source and retainer of all knowledge.

When the sacred scriptures thus came out in the open, the wily asura, Hayagreeva, who was on the look-out for such an opportunity, stole the Vedas and hid in pataal. Brahma became anxious to retrieve the Vedas. But neither he nor Satyavrata had it in them to tackle the mighty asura. So, both of them invoked Viṣṇu Bhagwan. Granting them their prayers, Viṣṇu assured them that pralaya was at hand and He would appear during that time as Matsya (Sanskrit for 'fish') avatar to retrieve the Vedas from Hayagreeva.

Not many days had passed when one fine morning, as Satyavrata was bathing in the river Kirtimal, a tiny fish got stuck in his upraised hands. The king had made his oblations and wanted to depart from the scene, but the fish pleaded with him to stay back lest the bigger fishes should eat it up. Then, the fish grew larger and larger by the moment, till it could be accommodated only in the vastness of the ocean.

It then dawned on the king that before him was none other than Matsyāvatāra. The avatar told him that the world would be submerged in water within seven days. But he need not be afraid as the Saptaṛṣi – the seven sages presiding over the epoch, would appear in a boat to take him on board. A strong rope and a serpent would also be at hand. Satyavrata should tie one end of the rope to the horn of the Matsya and the other to the tail of the serpent. Guided by the rope, the boat would go round and round the earth during the pralaya, giving him enough opportunity to witness the world-changing event in the company of the Saptaṛṣi. So, he should devote the available time collecting the seeds of every plant and herb and save them by sowing them in the earth when the deluge was over.

It happened precisely as Lord Viṣṇu in the form of Matsya had said. After a lapse of seven days, there was nothing but water to be seen in all directions. When the king began to drown, the Saptarṣi pulled him onto the boat. The Matsya went to Pataal Loka and retrieved the Vedas after killing the asura Hayagreeva.

The Vedas are the source of knowledge of the world and Brahma uses this knowledge at the time of creation. At the time of dissolution, the knowledge remains dormant in the universe. All the seeds of the world and its knowledge are retained for creation to happen again. Creation and Dissolution are a leela or play of the Divine.

In dissolution, there is Silence.

We are designed to experience the silence in the four ways of pralaya.

1. Constant dissolution
2. Occasional dissolution
3. Material dissolution
4. Final dissolution

CONSTANT DISSOLUTION

At a gross body level, millions of cells in our body die every second.

At the subtle body level, emotions, thoughts, and desires which make up our ego, come up and recede all the time.

At the end of every thought or emotion, there is silence. This reabsorption of the ego into silence is an automatic process and is always happening.

How can we consciously dissolve the ego into Silence?

FIND THE SILENCE BETWEEN THOUGHTS

Look around in your room. What do you see?

You may see various objects- tables, clocks, chairs, beds, wardrobes, fans, etc.

What do we see between all these objects, Space? If you blur out the objects in the room, all you will see is space. The objects are in space.

Similarly, the room of our minds is filled with thoughts as objects. In between the thoughts, there is space. If you blur out the thoughts, there is only space.

In the space you will find silence. In the silence you can be in touch with yourSelf.

Whenever the mind is overactive, just blur the objects in the mind, find the gap between the thoughts, and in the bliss of silence, the ego shall recede.

DISSOLUTION INTO SILENCE DURING SLEEP.

There is the dissolution of the world that happens at the end of the day, when one goes into silence in a deep sleep state.

Have you noticed that when your body or mind has been overworked and stressed out, deep sleep can rejuvenate you completely? In the silence of the deep sleep, the body and mind heal.

We go to sleep every day, yet we never get bored with it. We feel fulfilled and content if we sleep well.

When we go into deep sleep, we touch the bliss layer - the anandamaya kosha. We experience deep silence in deep sleep.

Do you have trouble getting into deep sleep?

Make sure you spend the last few minutes before you sleep winding down.

You can say a few prayers.

Let go of any agitation that still lingers from the day.

Think of the day and say

- Sorry if I hurt anybody today knowingly or unknowingly.
- I forgive those that hurt me knowingly or unknowingly.
- Thank you for all that I am blessed with.

I am filled with Love.

Did you know?

When one's mind is overworked, one cannot touch the deep sleep state easily due to the chatter in the mind.

Silence your overworked mind through chants or by focusing on your breath for at least 10 minutes before you go to sleep.

THE FALSE REALITY OF DREAM

Once, a wood-cutter lay dreaming when someone woke him up. Greatly annoyed, he said, "Why have you disturbed my sleep? I was dreaming of myself as a king and as the father of seven children. The princes were becoming well-versed in military arts. I was on my throne, ruling over my subjects."

"Why have you demolished my world of joy? Fool!!" said the wood-cutter.

"But that was a mere dream", said the other man. The woodcutter replied, 'You do not understand. I becoming a king in the dream was just as real as me being a woodcutter. If being a wood-cutter is real, then being a king in the dream is also real. If the dream is not real, then I being a woodcutter is also not real."

Do I reside in the mind or the Self through my waking hours? If I operate from the mind, it is a dream and unreal. Only the Self is real.

Silence at the End of Life

What happens when one leaves the body at the time of death?

When one dies, the subtle body leaves the gross body.

The gross body disintegrates and dissolves into the Universe. The body becomes part of the earth, the Vāyu from the body becomes one with the universal Vāyu, Jal, one with the universal Jal, and the fire dissipates.

The conscious mind or the manomaya kosha, becomes dormant.

The prana carries the Jiva along with its Vāsanās, out of the body.

The Jiva in its subtle body, moves from one gross body to another.

There is silence between two lives. In this silence, too, there is freedom and healing.

Death is not an end. It is just a new beginning.

This is a temporary dissolution too. The Jiva continues to exist.

TREE OF LIFE

When a leaf becomes old, dry, and falls off a tree, it decays into the soil and is absorbed back into the tree, only to form another leaf or fruit or bark of the tree.

The tree existed before the leaf, with the leaf, and after the leaf too.

The Jiva too takes a different form and name in the next life.

MOKSHA- DISSOLUTION OF THE INDIVIDUAL "I" INTO SILENCE

When the Vāsanās are completely sublimed, the individual identity of "I" is dissolved. There is no material (Vāsanās) to be condensed into a subtle body and gross body and hence this is permanent dissolution.

As a salt doll dissolves into water to become one with the water, the Jiva dissolves into the Supreme Consciousness to experience oneness.

Like a river that merges into the ocean, the Jiva merges into the Supreme Consciousness to have no individual existence.

This permanent, deep, steady silence is called Mukti, Moksha, Nirvana or Kaivalya in the various scriptures.

"When one leaves the body before Vāsanā's die, it is Mrutyu (death).

When the Vāsanā's die before one leaves the body, it is Mukti (Total Freedom)

In this state there is no individuality, there is only oneness, there is only One."

-N.V. Raghuramji

SILENCE, THE DOORWAY TO LOVE

When one goes beyond the chatter of the mind, to just "Be" in silence, one experiences freedom.

In the deepest caves of Silence, there is Supreme Love.

The experience of Love is our recognition of our shared being.

Love is not a mere emotion. It is the Supreme Being.

The seed of Love sprouts in Silence...

It grows in Silence...

It bears fruit in Silence...

It ripens in Silence...

It is tasted in Silence...

It pollinates in Silence...

It spreads in Silence...

It is planted in Silence...

It breathes in Silence...

Silence is the Source of everything

In the Silence, is Self...

This silence leads one to the cause...

This Silence leads to the destination- The Supreme Love

Supreme Love is peace, knowledge, and THE ONE...

One begins in Silence, lives and survives in Silence, and finally merges in Silence with the Supreme Consciousness.

- **Muraliji**

अहमात्मा गुडाकेश सर्वभूताशयस्थितः |
अहमादिश्च मध्यं च भूतानामन्त एव च ||

aham ātmā guḍākeśha sarva-bhūtāśhaya-sthitaḥ
aham ādiśh cha madhyaṁ cha bhūtānām anta eva cha

O Arjun, I am seated in the heart of all living entities. I am the beginning, middle, and end of all beings.

- **Bhagavad Gītā Chapter 10 Verse 20**

VATAPATRA SHAYI

Vatapatra Shayi - the child Kṛṣṇa floating on a ficus leaf - is a symbolic representation of the first form of life on earth (or the only form of life). He is the representation of the Supreme Consciousness that is present before creation, during creation and after creation. The entire earth remains under water for millions of years.

The child form of Viṣṇu (Kṛṣṇa) on a Ficus Leaf, which is known as Vatapatra, lies on the ocean of Consciousness.

This wonderful incident is mentioned in the Mārkaṇḍeya Purāṇa.

Ṛṣi Mārkaṇḍeya was blessed to witness the final dissolution. The Ṛṣi saw destruction all around. Water submerged everything. For millions of years, there was only water all around the Ṛṣi. Finally, he noticed the Vatapatra Shayi-Kṛṣṇa floating on the Ficus leaf. Child Kṛṣṇa was lying on the leaf sucking his toe.

When Mārkaṇḍeya went near, the baby took a breath and the Ṛṣi was sucked in. Inside, the Ṛṣi witnessed thousands of universes and myriad living forms. When the baby exhaled, the Ṛṣi came back to the ocean of consciousness. This continued to happen with every breath of Vātapattraśāyi.

All creation exists in the Divine. When the Divine breathes in, one becomes part of the world; when the Divine breathes out, one enters the silence of the dissolution, where there is nothing but the Supreme Self.

WHERE HUMILITY MEETS GREATNESS

In the silence of the mind and body, one awakens to the greatness of the Supreme Being.

When the river of individuality "I" surrenders to the ocean of "Consciousness", there is humility.

Humility comes from recognising and revering the Divinity of the Supreme.

In the epic Rāmāyaṇa, Hanuman's leap across the ocean to Lanka, is not just a marvel of strength, it's a soaring example of humility, devotion, and selfless service.

Though Hanuman possesses immense powers, strength, speed, intellect, and fearlessness, he never uses them to glorify himself. His every action is anchored in one purpose: service to Lord Rāma.

Here's what Hanuman's flight teaches us:

1. Selfless Service

Hanuman's mission is to find Sīta; not for fame, not for reward, but out of pure devotion. His actions are not about *him*; they are about the *divine*.

True greatness begins when the thought of "I", "me", and "mine" steps aside.

2. Humility in Power

Despite his supernatural abilities, Hanuman never boasts. He acts with quiet strength and unwavering humility, always attributing his success to Rāma's grace.

Humility is not a weakness; it is the highest strength.

3. Overcoming the Impossible

The vast ocean before him is no small obstacle. Yet, powered by devotion, he leaps without hesitation.

When the purpose is pure, even the impossible becomes possible.

4. Inner Strength

Hanuman's might is not just physical; it flows from the wellspring of his inner conviction and unwavering faith.

Real power comes not from muscles, but from conviction.

5. The Absence of Ego

Even after burning down Lanka and returning victorious, Hanuman remains humble, never seeking praise.

Ego shrinks us. Humility and reverence expand us.

In essence, Hanuman's journey to Lanka is not just a physical leap — it is a spiritual ascent.

A reminder that true power lies not in what we can *do*, but in *why* we do it.

WHEN OUR ACTIONS ARE ROOTED IN LOVE, SERVICE, AND HUMILITY — WE TOO SOAR TO THE INFINITE SKY.

Nasadiya Sukta of Rig Veda

ON ORIGIN OF THE UNIVERSE

Neither existence nor nonexistence was there
Neither matter nor space around
What covered it, where it was and who protected?
Why, that plasma, all pervading, deep and profound?

Neither death nor immortality was there
And there was neither day nor night
But for that breathless one breathing on its own
There was nothing else, surely nothing

It was darkness concealed in darkness
And an uninterrupted continuum of fluid
Out came in material form and shape
That one lying deep inside, on its own intent.

In the cosmic mind, all pervading
Desire, the primal seed made its first appearance
And the wise men, seeking deep in their heart
Could see the link between 'that is' and 'that is not'.

Reins of the link, a grid of crisscross lines,
Holds all the seeds and mighty forces,
Microcosmic forces within
And macro forces out above.
Who really knows, who can declare

When it started or where from?
And where will the creation end?
Seekers and sought entered later -
And so, who knows when all this manifested?

That one, out of which the creation came
May hold the reins or not,
Perceiving all from above, That one alone
Knows the beginning - may not know too.

CONCLUSIONS

All our lives, we tend to believe that what we see and hear is *the truth*. We react to people's words and actions, including our own, and quickly judge ourselves, others, and the world.

But what we see is just the surface, shaped by our senses, our thoughts, our moods, and even our past experiences. It's like wearing tinted glasses: everything looks a certain way because of the lens we're looking through.

Reality, though, is deeper. It doesn't change with our moods or opinions. The Upanishads call this *Brahman*, the real, infinite essence of truth behind everything. The world we see is like a movie projected on a screen - beautiful, emotional, but not the whole truth.

So, when we say *"perception dissolves into reality"*, it means shifting from:

- Seeing with our eyes to understanding with wisdom
- Mistaking a rope for a snake in the dark, to realising it was just a rope
- Thinking "I'm just this body and mind" to knowing "I am something far greater, pure awareness."

Every day, as you relate with the world and the people in it, every moment ask yourself, **"Where am I? Stuck in my mind-movie, or aligned with the Cosmic Script?"**

For comments or questions on the book please write to

arthikrish@gmail.com.